INSTANT POT®
COOKBOOK

GOOD
HOUSEKEEPING

INSTANT POT®
COOKBOOK

60 DELICIOUS FOOLPROOF RECIPES

★ GOOD FOOD GUARANTEED ★

HEARST
books

HEARSTBOOKS

An Imprint of Sterling Publishing Co., Inc.
1166 Avenue of the Americas
New York, NY 10036

ISBN 978-1-61837-252-9

The Good Housekeeping Cookbook Seal guarantees that the recipes in this publication meet the strict standards
of the Good Housekeeping Research Institute. The Institute has been a source of reliable information and a consumer
advocate since 1900, and established its seal of approval in 1909. Every recipe in this publication has been
triple-tested for ease, reliability, and great taste by the Institute.

Distributed in Canada by Sterling Publishing Co., Inc.
c/o Canadian Manda Group, 664 Annette Street
Toronto, Ontario M6S 2C8, Canada
Distributed in Australia by NewSouth Books
45 Beach Street, Coogee NSW 2034, Australia

For information about custom editions, special sales, and premium and corporate purchases, please contact
Sterling Special Sales at 800-805-5489 or specialsales@sterlingpublishing.com.

Manufactured in Canada

8 10 9 7

sterlingpublishing.com
goodhousekeeping.com
For photography credits, see page 126

CONTENTS

Smoky Vegan Black Bean Soup
(page 50)

Foreword

The Instant Pot® has gained quite a cult-following. Busy parents, working professionals, and avid cooks all agree—it's life changing. With such a hefty claim, we brought the multicooker into our trusted Good Housekeeping Kitchen Appliances and Technology Lab.

Alongside nine other multicookers, we tested 18 cups of dry rice, 68 pounds of meat, and 44 pounds of veggies. We pressure cooked and slow cooked beef stew. We evaluated the cooker's ability to evenly brown meat and make rice. We assessed how quickly the cookers came to pressure. And after all that, we understand the Instant Pot® obsession.

The Instant Pot® is a one-pot wonder. One of the buzziest additions to the Good Housekeeping Test Kitchen, this all-in-one appliance allows you to cook weeknight meals that taste like they have been braised for hours. Long gone are the days of fear-filled pressure cooking! With the Instant Pot® you can create a variety of meals without a worry.

In this book we have partnered with Instant Pot® to create delicious triple-tested recipes in the GH Test Kitchens. I know that trying a new device can be a little daunting, so our introduction derived from the Instant Pot® manual provides easy-to-use instructions that will ensure great results.

Need a place to start? Try our Weeknight Tuscan Ragu, Chipotle Lentil Chili, or No-Time Tikka Masala. Each of these dishes normally requires hours of cooking on the stovetop, but with the Instant Pot®, these flavorful favorites are ready in less than an hour. Think risotto is too much for a weeknight? Combine the ingredients for Butternut Squash Risotto in the pot and within 30 minutes it's done. No stirring required.

Think you might miss your slow cooker? No worries! The Instant Pot® boasts a slow cooking function (among other functions like yogurt making and rice cooking) so you can still cook all of your tried-and-true favorites. I'm a big fan of Brisket with Roasted Red Onions. The Cajun Beef & Grits make great use of the sauté function, too. Or maybe you're in the mood for New Mexican Green Chile Pork—save any leftovers for a great filling for tacos the next day!

Each time I use the Instant Pot®, I am amazed by the results. Let our *Instant Pot® Cookbook* be your guide to making delicious, crowd-pleasing, and convenient meals. Toss together a few ingredients, press a few buttons, and enjoy.

SUSAN WESTMORELAND
Food Director, *Good Housekeeping*

The Instant Pot® Guide:
WHAT IS THE INSTANT POT®?

The Instant Pot® is a multicooker that combines the benefits of multiple kitchen appliances in one space-saving kitchen machine. It functions as a pressure cooker and slow cooker, along with a sauté pan, rice cooker, yogurt maker, and steamer. It also has a function that keeps your prepared meal warm, and newer models include other features as well. With a press of a button, the Instant Pot® has simplified everyday cooking by reducing cooking times and ensuring nutritious meals are on the table even faster.

INSTANT POT® PREPARATION

Before using the Instant Pot®, make sure to follow these procedures.

1. Install the condensation collector at the rear of the cooker. Place the steam release handle on the lid.

2. To remove the lid, hold the handle, turn the lid counterclockwise, and lift.

3. Remove the inner pot from the cooker, unless using the Sauté function. If using this function, the next steps can proceed with the inner pot in the cooker.

4. Add food and liquids to the inner pot as the recipe directs. If steaming, place the steamer rack on the bottom of the inner pot first.

5. Wipe the outside of the inner pot dry. Make sure there is no food debris on the cooking element.

6. Put the inner pot back into the cooker. Rotate slightly to ensure that it is seated correctly.

7. Make sure the sealing ring is properly seated in the sealing ring rack and there is no deformations. Do not attempt to repair a deformed ring rack.

8. To place lid, reverse step 1. Place the lid on the cooker, align the ▲ mark on the lid with the unlock mark and turn clockwise.

PRESSURE COOKING IN THE INSTANT POT®

Unlike your grandmother's stovetop pressure cooker, which had an unsafe reputation, the Instant Pot® is designed to avoid common user errors and safety hazards of conventional pressure cooking. Follow these procedures each time for proven results.

1. Connect the power cord. The LED display shows "OFF" indicating that it's in the standby state. Follow the Instant Pot® Preparation steps.

2. Select a cooking program like Manual/Pressure Cook, Soup, Meat/Stew, Beans/Chili, etc. The steam release handle should be in Sealing position. Once a program key is pressed, its indicator lights up. Within 10 seconds after pressing a program key, you can still select other program keys and adjust cooking time.

3. Select cooking pressure. All programs besides Rice default to high pressure. The Rice program defaults to low pressure. Low pressure operates at half of the regular working pressure and can be used to avoid overcooking tender food such as vegetables.

4. Select the cooking time. You may use the Adjust key (except for Manual/Pressure Cook and Rice programs) to adjust cooking time.

Press the Adjust key repeatedly to change between Normal, Less, and More modes, which will light up on the display. If necessary, change the cooking time with [+] and [-]. Press and hold the [+] or [-] key for faster changes.

5. Cooking starts automatically 10 seconds after the last key press. Three audible beeps will sound to indicate the cooking process has begun. The LED display shows "ON" indicating that the pre-heating state is in progress. Once the cooker reaches working pressure, the LED display changes from "ON" to the programmed cooking time. The cooking time counts down to indicate the remaining time in minutes.

6. When the pressure-cooking cycle finishes, the cooker beeps and automatically goes into the Keep Warm cycle. The Keep Warm cycle can be used for up to 10 hours. After 10 hours, the cooker goes into standby state.

Press Keep Warm/Cancel to stop the cycle and return the pot to its standby state.

RELEASING PRESSURE

There are two methods of releasing pressure when using the Instant Pot®.

Quick Release: Turn the steam release handle to the Venting position to let steam out until the float valve drops down. Never pull out the steam release handle while releasing steam as escaping steam is extremely hot and can cause scalds. For food with large liquid volume or starch content, use Natural Release instead as thick liquid may splatter out.

Natural Release: Allow the cooker to cool down naturally until the float valve drops down. This may take 10 to 40 minutes, or even more, depending on the amount of food in the cooker. Place a wet towel on the lid to speed up cooling.

SLOW COOKING IN THE INSTANT POT®

1. Connect the power cord. The LCD displays "OFF," indicating that the cooker is in the standby state. Follow the Instant Pot® Preparation (see page 9).

2. Select the Slow Cook program. The steam release handle should be in the Venting position.

3. Change the cooking time between 30 minutes and 20 hours pressing the [+] or [-] key.

4. Select the desired cooking mode with the Adjust key. By pushing the Adjust key repeatedly, you can adjust the cooking programs (see pages 12–13.)

5. Cooking starts automatically in 10 seconds after the last key is pressed. Three audible beeps will sound to indicate the cooking process has begun. The LED display shows "ON" indicating that the pre-heating state is in progress.

6. When the cooking finishes, the cooker beeps and automatically goes into the Keep Warm cycle for 10 hours.

SAUTÉING IN THE INSTANT POT®

1. Connect the power cord. The LCD displays "OFF," indicating that the cooker is in the standby state.

2. Select the Sauté program. To change the cooking temperature, press the Sauté program key repeatedly to select between Normal, Less, and More. (See Cooking Program Options for more detail).

3. The preheating cycle starts automatically in 10 seconds after the last key is pressed. Three audible beeps will sound to indicate the working temperature is reached. The LED display shows "HOT" indicating you can add food to the inner pot.

4. When you have finished sautéing the food, press Cancel. The LCD displays "OFF," indicating the cooker is in the standby state.

Instant Pot® Safety Tips

When pressure cooking with the Instant Pot® there are important safety tips to keep in mind.

- Do not open the Instant Pot® until the cooker has cooled and all internal pressure has been released. If the float valve is still up or the lid is difficult to turn, it is an indication that the cooker is still pressurized. Do not force it open.
- Make sure the steam release valve is in the Sealing position for all the pressure-cooking programs.
- Always check the steam release valve, float valve and anti-block shield for clogging before use.
- For all pressure-cooking programs, the total amount of pre-cooked food and liquid in the inner pot should not pass the ⅔ line. When cooking food that expands during cooking such as rice, beans or vegetables, the inner pot should not pass the ½ line.
- Be aware that certain foods, such as applesauce, cranberries, pearl barley, oatmeal and other cereals, split peas, noodles, macaroni, rhubarb, and spaghetti can foam, froth, sputter, and clog the steam release. We do not recommend cooking these dishes under pressure but they can be made using the Slow Cook function.

Cooking Program Options

Depending on the model of your Instant Pot® there are a variety of pre-programed buttons for easy use. These are the most common programs.

PROGRAM	MODE	COOKING OPTION	NOTES
Bean & Chili	Less	Less soft texture	Choose different modes based on the desired bean texture.
	Normal	Soft texture	
	More	Very soft texture	
Egg	Less	Soft-boiled eggs	Pre-set times are intended for extra large eggs. Adjust cooking time to account for different size eggs.
	Normal	Medium-boiled eggs	
	More	Hard-boiled eggs	
Meat & Stew	Less	Use for soft meat texture	Choose different modes based on the desired meat texture.
	Normal	Use for very soft meat texture	
	More	Use for fall-off-the-bone meat texture	
Multigrain	Less	Wild rice, brown rice, mung beans, etc	Choose the less or normal mode based on the type of grain and desired texture.
	Normal	Wild rice, brown rice, mung beans, etc	
	More	Tough grains or a mixture of grains and beans	In newer models, this program includes 45 minutes of warm water soaking time prior to 60 minutes of pressure cooking.

PROGRAM	MODE	COOKING OPTION	NOTES
Rice	Less	Al dente white rice	This is an automated cooking program. The LCD display will show "AUTO" until cooking count-down time starts.
	Normal	Normal texture white rice	
	More	Softer texture white rice	
Sauté	Less	Simmering, thickening, and reducing liquids	Safety is important. Never have the lid on while sautéing. And after 30 minutes the pot will turn off to the standby state.
	Normal	Pan searing or sautéing	
	More	Stir-frying or browning	
Slow Cook	Less	Corresponds to LOW setting in a temperature-controlled slow cooker	As a non-pressure-cooking program, you may also use the Instant Pot® glass lid as an option.
	Normal	Corresponds to a MEDIUM setting in a temperature-controlled slow cooker	
	More	Corresponds to a HIGH setting in a temperature-controlled slow cooker	
Soup & Broth	Less	Use for soup without meat	The soup/broth will remain clear due to lack of boiling motion under pressure cooking.
	Normal	Use for soup with meat	
	More	Use for rich bone broth	
Steam	Less	Use for vegetables	Use the trivet provided to elevate the food above water. The Quick release method should be used to prevent food from overcooking.
	Normal	Use for fish and seafood	
	More	Use for meat	

Devilish Eggs
(page 23)

1 | Basic Recipes

The Instant Pot® is a great tool to use when stocking your pantry with homemade sauces and stocks. A pro at extracting intense flavors, the Instant Pot® uses its pressure-cooker settings to develop robust flavors. Put your stockpot away and throw the makings for chicken, beef, or vegetable broth right in. In half the traditional time you will have a beautiful broth for a soup base or as an ingredient in other recipes. But it can do more! Homemade marinara and applesauce are easy and avoid processed ingredients that are in many store-bought varieties. And you'll love our easy take on the classic hard-boiled egg with deviled-egg variations.

PRESSURE COOKER
Chicken Broth

Nothing beats the flavor of homemade chicken broth. Make it in large batches and freeze in containers for up to four months. Our recipe has an added bonus: The cooked chicken can be used in casseroles and salads.

ACTIVE TIME: 10 MINUTES   **TOTAL TIME:** 40 MINUTES, PLUS COOLING   **MAKES:** 7½ CUPS

3½ pounds chicken parts (such as wings, backs, legs)

2 carrots, cut into 2-inch pieces

1 stalk celery, cut into 2-inch pieces

1 medium onion, quartered (see Tip)

5 sprigs fresh parsley

1 clove garlic, smashed with side of chef's knife

½ teaspoon dried thyme

1 bay leaf

1 In Instant Pot®, combine chicken, carrots, celery, onion, parsley, garlic, thyme, bay leaf, and 6 cups water.

2 Cover and lock lid. Select Manual/Pressure Cook and cook at high for 30 minutes. Once cooking is wcomplete, release pressure by using natural release function.

3 Strain broth through colander into large bowl; discard solids. Strain again through sieve into containers; cool. Cover and refrigerate to use within 3 days, or freeze for up to 4 months.

4 To use, skim and discard fat from surface of broth.

EACH CUP: ABOUT 40 CALORIES, 5G PROTEIN, 5G CARBOHYDRATE, 0G TOTAL FAT (0G SATURATED), 0G FIBER, 48MG SODIUM.

TIP

There is no need to peel the onion. Leaving the skin on will add a golden color to the chicken broth.

PRESSURE COOKER
Vegetable Broth

For an Asian-flavored broth, add minced lemongrass,
minced fresh ginger, or chopped fresh cilantro.

ACTIVE TIME: 25 MINUTES **TOTAL TIME:** 40 MINUTES **MAKES:** 8 CUPS

4 large leeks, white and pale green parts only

1 small fennel bulb, trimmed and cut into 1-inch pieces

3 large carrots, peeled and sliced

3 stalks celery with leaves, cut into 1-inch chunks

2 parsnips, peeled and sliced

4 ounces mushrooms, trimmed and halved

1 large tomato, cut into 1-inch chunks

4 cloves garlic, smashed with side of chef's knife

10 sprigs fresh parsley

4 sprigs fresh thyme

2 bay leaves

1 teaspoon whole black peppercorns

¾ teaspoon salt

1 Thinly slice leeks. Rinse leeks in large bowl of cold water, swishing to remove sand; transfer to colander to drain, leaving sand in bottom of bowl.

2 In Instant Pot®, combine leeks, fennel, carrots, celery, parsnips, mushrooms, tomato, garlic, parsley, thyme, bay leaves, peppercorns, and 8 cups water. Cover and lock lid. Select Manual/Pressure Cook and cook at high pressure for 15 minutes. Once cooking is complete, release pressure by using natural release function.

3 Strain broth through colander into large bowl; discard solids. Stir in salt. Pour broth into containers and cool. Cover and refrigerate to use within 3 days, or freeze for up to 4 months.

EACH CUP: ABOUT 15 CALORIES, 0G PROTEIN, 2G CARBOHYDRATE, 0G TOTAL FAT (0G SATURATED), 0G FIBER, 229MG SODIUM.

PRESSURE COOKER
Brown Beef Stock

For a richer, meatier flavor, switch it up and use one pound of beef bones and three pounds of meaty neck bones, beef shanks, or oxtails.

ACTIVE TIME: 10 MINUTES   **TOTAL TIME:** 3 HOURS, 15 MINUTES   **MAKES:** 9 CUPS

2   pounds beef bones, cut into 3-inch pieces
2   pounds meaty neck bones or beef shanks
2   medium onions, halved
3   carrots, halved crosswise
2   stalks celery, halved crosswise
1   small bunch parsley
1   bay leaf
½   teaspoon dried thyme

1 Preheat oven to 450°F. Spread beef bones, onions, carrots, and celery in large roasting pan (17½ x 11½ inches). Roast, stirring every 15 minutes, until well browned, about 1 hour. Transfer browned bones and vegetables to Instant Pot®.

2 Carefully pour off fat from roasting pan. On stovetop, add 1 cup water to roasting pan and heat to boiling, stirring until browned bits are loosened from bottom of pan; add to pot. Add 8 cups water, parsley, bay leaf, and thyme.

3 Cover and lock lid. Select Manual/Pressure Cook and cook at high pressure for 1 hour. Once cooking is complete, release pressure by using natural release function.

4 Strain broth through colander into large bowl; discard solids. Strain again through fine-mesh sieve into containers. Cool. Cover and refrigerate to use within 3 days, or freeze for up to 4 months. To use, skim and discard fat from surface of stock.

EACH CUP: ABOUT 30 CALORIES, 5G PROTEIN, 3G CARBOHYDRATE, 0G TOTAL FAT (0G SATURATED), 0G FIBER, 48MG SODIUM.

PRESSURE COOKER
Marinara Sauce

Two variations on the classic sauce add extra flavor
and heat to our go-to base recipe.

ACTIVE TIME: 5 MINUTES   TOTAL TIME: 40 MINUTES   MAKES: 7 CUPS

- 1   onion, chopped
- 3   cloves garlic, finely chopped
- 3   tablespoons olive oil
- 2   cans (28 ounces each) plum tomatoes in puree
- ¼   cup tomato paste
- ½   teaspoon salt
- ¼   cup chopped fresh basil or parsley (optional)

1   In Instant Pot® using sauté function, cook onion and garlic in oil, uncovered, for 4 minutes, or until softening. Hit cancel to turn off sauté function. Add tomatoes, tomato paste, and salt to pot. Break up tomatoes with potato masher.

2   Cover and lock lid. Select Manual/Pressure Cook and cook at high pressure for 20 minutes. Once cooking is complete, release pressure by using quick release. Stir in basil (if using). Let stand 5 minutes for flavors to absorb. Stir well to break up tomatoes if desired.

3   Freeze sauce for up to 6 months.

EACH ½ CUP: 60 CALORIES, 1G PROTEIN, 6G CARBOHYDRATE, 3G TOTAL FAT (0G SATURATED), 1G FIBER, 319MG SODIUM.

Arrabbiata Sauce

Prepare as directed above, but add **¼ to ½ teaspoon crushed red pepper flakes** with onion and garlic in step 1. Proceed as directed and omit basil.

EACH ½ CUP: 60 CALORIES, 1G PROTEIN, 6G CARBOHYDRATE, 3G TOTAL FAT (0G SATURATED), 1G FIBER, 319MG SODIUM.

Spaghetti all'Amatriciana

In Instant Pot® using sauté function, cook **4 ounces chopped pancetta** in **1 tablespoon oil**, uncovered, for 5 minutes, or until crisped. Pour off excess fat. Add **onion, garlic**, and **¼ to ½ teaspoon crushed red pepper flakes** and cook for 4 minutes, as directed. Hit cancel to turn off sauté function. Omit tomato paste and basil and proceed as directed. Divide in half; use 1 batch to coat **1 pound pasta** (4 main-dish servings) and add ⅓ **cup chopped fresh parsley**.

EACH SERVING: 560 CALORIES, 19G PROTEIN, 96G CARBOHYDRATE, 9G TOTAL FAT (2G SATURATED), 7G FIBER, 629MG SODIUM.

Easy-Peel Hard-Boiled Eggs

Pressure cooking makes easy work of peeling hard-boiled eggs.

ACTIVE TIME: 5 MINUTES   **TOTAL TIME:** 10 MINUTES, PLUS CHILLING   **MAKES:** 6 SERVINGS

6 large eggs

Place eggs on a rack or steamer basket in Instant Pot®. Add 1 cup water. Cover and lock lid. Select Manual/Pressure Cook and cook at high pressure for 5 minutes. Once cooking is complete, release pressure by using a quick release. Transfer to bowl to cool and store refrigerated for up to 3 days.

EACH SERVING: ABOUT 70 CALORIES, 6G PROTEIN, 0G CARBOHYDRATE, 5G TOTAL FAT (2G SATURATED), 0G FIBER, 70MG SODIUM.

Beet- Dyed Eggs

In medium saucepan, combine **8 cups water**, **4 medium beets** (peeled and thinly sliced), **2 cups distilled white vinegar**, and **1 tablespoon salt** and bring to boiling on high. Reduce heat to simmering; cook 20 minutes. Cool liquid completely. Remove and reserve beets for another use. Transfer pickling liquid to gallon-size resealable bag set in large bowl; add **12 peeled hard-boiled eggs**. Squeeze air out of bag and seal, making sure eggs are submerged. Refrigerate 1 hour. Remove eggs from liquid and blot completely dry with paper towels before using.

TIP

The Beet-Dyed Eggs can be used when making Horseradish Beet Devilish Eggs.

Devilish Eggs

These 5 variations are devilish and delish! To prep, peel and halve 12 large hard-boiled eggs lengthwise. Transfer yolks to medium bowl and mash with a choice of flavoring below. Pipe mixture into whites and garnish as directed.

HORSERADISH BEET

3 tablespoons mayonnaise + cup very well drained prepared horseradish + 1 tablespoon Worcestershire sauce + teaspoon salt.

Pipe into Beet-Dyed Egg whites (see facing page); garnish with fresh dill.

. . . .

CAESAR

½ cup mayonnaise + ¼ cup grated Parmesan cheese + 2 tablespoons lemon juice + 2 teaspoons Dijon mustard + 1 small clove garlic, crushed with garlic press.

Garnish filled eggs with broken Parmesan crisps, pepper, and fresh basil.

. . . .

GUACAMOLE

1 small avocado + ¼ cup mayonnaise + ¼ cup finely chopped fresh cilantro + 1 very small shallot, finely chopped + 2 tablespoons lime juice + ½ teaspoon salt.

Garnish filled eggs with broken tortilla chips and thinly sliced serrano chiles.

MISO-GINGER

½ cup mayonnaise + 2 tablespoons white or yellow miso + 1 teaspoon grated peeled fresh ginger + ½ teaspoon ground black pepper + ¼ teaspoon sugar.

Garnish filled eggs with snipped chives and finely julienned fresh ginger.

. . . .

HAM & CHEESE

½ cup mayonnaise + ½ cup finely grated sharp Cheddar cheese + 3 tablespoons drained sweet relish + 2 slices deli ham, finely chopped + 1 tablespoon spicy brown mustard + ¼ teaspoon salt.

Spicy Curry Lentils
(page 34)

2 | Beans & Grains

Wonderfully filling but often requiring long cooking times, dried beans and grains are prepared in a flash when using the Instant Pot®. Whether served as a side, a component in a dish, or as a vegetarian main course, our trusted recipes for lentils, black-eyed peas, long-grain rice, and more deliver great flavor. Plus, delicious creamy Italian rice dishes like Risotto Milanese and Butternut Squash Risotto are made under pressure quickly and easily. And by using the pressure-cooker function, you will reduce your time over the stove, allowing more time to enjoy these dishes with loved ones around the kitchen table.

PRESSURE COOKER
Campfire Baked Beans

Though bacon adds a smoky, meaty flavor, it can be omitted for a vegetarian option.

ACTIVE TIME: 15 MINUTES   **TOTAL TIME:** 30 MINUTES   **MAKES:** 8 (½ CUP) SERVINGS

1   cup ketchup

¼   cup molasses

4   teaspoons mustard powder

½   teaspoon ground black pepper

3   slices thick-cut bacon, chopped

1   medium onion, chopped

1   small green bell pepper, chopped

3   cans (15 ounces each) lower-sodium navy beans, rinsed and drained

2   teaspoons apple cider vinegar

1 In medium bowl, whisk together ketchup, molasses, mustard, and black pepper.

2 In Instant Pot® using sauté function, cook bacon, onion, and bell pepper, uncovered, for 6 minutes, or until bacon crisps. Hit cancel to turn off sauté function. Pour off any excess fat.

3 Stir in beans. Spoon ketchup mixture on top; do not stir. Cover and lock lid. Select Manual/Pressure Cook and cook at high pressure for 8 minutes. Once cooking is complete, release pressure by using natural release function. Stir in vinegar and let stand at least 5 minutes for flavors to absorb.

EACH SERVING: ABOUT 225 CALORIES, 11G PROTEIN, 45G CARBOHYDRATE, 2G TOTAL FAT (0G SATURATED), 8G FIBER, 532MG SODIUM.

PRESSURE COOKER
Hoppin' John

This delicious rice and black-eyed pea mixture is
served in the South on New Year's Day for luck:
The peas represent coins, ensuring a prosperous year.

ACTIVE TIME: 20 MINUTES **TOTAL TIME:** 1 HOUR **MAKES:** 16 (½ CUP) SERVINGS

1½ cups dried black-eyed peas, rinsed and picked over

1 large smoked ham hock (12 ounces)

1 large onion (12 ounces), chopped

4 cloves garlic, finely chopped

1 bay leaf

½ teaspoon dried thyme

¾ teaspoon salt

4 slices bacon, chopped

2 stalks celery, chopped

1 red bell pepper, chopped

1 cup regular long-grain rice

1 cup chicken broth, store-bought or homemade (page 17)

¼ teaspoon crushed red pepper flakes

2 tablespoons chopped fresh parsley

1 In Instant Pot®, combine black-eyed peas, ham hock, ¾ cup of the onion, 2 teaspoons of the garlic, bay leaf, thyme, and 4 cups water. Cover and lock lid. Select Manual/Pressure Cook and cook at high pressure for 20 minutes. Once cooking is complete, release pressure by using a quick release. Drain peas (and clean out pot). Reserve ham hock and discard bay leaf. Season peas with ½ teaspoon salt and gently stir to combine.

2 In pot using sauté function, cook bacon, uncovered, for 5 minutes, or until crisp, stirring occasionally. Remove bacon to plate. To drippings in pot, add remaining onion, the celery, and the bell pepper. Cook uncovered for 4 minutes, or until vegetables begin to soften, stirring occasionally. Hit cancel to turn off sauté function.

3 Stir in rice, chicken broth, pepper flakes, remaining garlic, remaining ¼ teaspoon salt, and ¾ cup water. Add ham hock, pushing it down into liquid. Cover and lock lid. Select Manual/Pressure Cook and cook at high pressure for 8 minutes. Once cooking is complete, release pressure by using a quick release.

4 From ham hock, remove meat and finely chop it. Discard the bone. Gently fold parsley, peas, ham, and bacon into rice mixture. Let stand 5 minutes before serving.

EACH SERVING: ABOUT 140 CALORIES, 6G PROTEIN, 22G CARBOHYDRATE, 3G TOTAL FAT (1G SATURATED), 4G FIBER, 239MG SODIUM.

TIP

Smoked ham hocks can be found in supermarkets alongside other pork products, and are usually sold in packages of two or three. Wrap unused hocks in heavy-duty foil and freeze for up to 6 months.

PRESSURE COOKER
Tuscan White Beans with Sage

Leave it to the Italians to give us flawlessly flavored beans.

ACTIVE TIME: 15 MINUTES   **TOTAL TIME:** 25 MINUTES, PLUS SOAKING BEANS   **MAKES:** 8 (¾ CUP) SERVINGS

1   package (16 ounces) dried white kidney beans (cannellini) or Great Northern beans

2   onions, sliced in half-rounds

3   tablespoons olive oil, plus more for serving

3   slices bacon

4   large cloves garlic, smashed with side of chef's knife

1   bay leaf

2   sprigs fresh sage leaves, plus 2 teaspoons thinly sliced sage

2   teaspoons salt

¼   teaspoon ground black pepper

1 Place beans in large bowl. Add cold water to cover by 2 inches. Let stand overnight. Drain and rinse well.

2 In Instant Pot® using sauté function, cook onion in oil, uncovered, for 4 minutes, or until softening. Hit cancel to turn off sauté function.

3 Add bacon, garlic, bay leaf, sage sprigs, drained beans, and 6 cups water. Cover and lock lid. Select Manual/Pressure Cook and cook at high pressure for 7 minutes. Once cooking is complete, release pressure by using a quick release.

4 Drain beans, reserving 1 cup cooking liquid. Discard bacon, sage sprigs, and bay leaf. Stir in salt, pepper, sliced sage, and ½ to 1 cup cooking liquid to desired consistency. (Note: You can use the leftover bean liquid as a base for soups or stews.) Serve hot, warm, or at room temperature. Drizzle with additional olive oil, if desired.

EACH SERVING: ABOUT 263 CALORIES, 14G PROTEIN, 37G CARBOHYDRATE, 7G TOTAL FAT (1G SATURATED), 20G FIBER, 617MG SODIUM.

TIP

An easy way to crush garlic is to use the side of a chef's knife. Place the knife on top of the clove and press down carefully using your palm. This releases the oils in the garlic and creates a subtle change in flavor.

PRESSURE COOKER
Parsley & Lemon Chickpeas

Fragrant lemon and parsley add brightness to this bean dish. Try serving these chickpeas alongside the Apricot-Braised Lamb Shanks (page 117).

ACTIVE TIME: 10 MINUTES **TOTAL TIME:** 1 HOUR, 15 MINUTES **MAKES:** 4 SERVINGS

1 medium onion, chopped

1 stalk celery, chopped

3 cloves garlic, smashed with side of chef's knife

3 tablespoons olive oil

1 cup dried chickpeas

1 can (14½ ounces) lower-sodium chicken broth or 1¾ cups homemade (page 17)

3 tablespoons finely chopped fresh parsley

½ teaspoon grated lemon zest

3 tablespoons lemon juice

½ teaspoon salt

⅛ teaspoon ground black pepper

1 In Instant Pot® using sauté function, cook onion, celery, and garlic, uncovered, in 1 tablespoon olive oil for 3 minutes, or until softening. Hit cancel to turn off sauté function.

2 Add chickpeas, broth, and ¾ cup water. Cover and lock lid. Select Manual/Pressure Cook and cook at high pressure for 40 minutes. Once cooking is complete, release pressure by using natural release function.

3 Drain chickpeas and discard garlic cloves. Toss in large bowl with parsley, lemon zest, lemon juice, salt, pepper, and remaining 2 tablespoons olive oil. Serve warm or room temperature. (Note: Recipe can be doubled, using the same cooking times.)

EACH SERVING: ABOUT 280 CALORIES, 10G PROTEIN, 33G CARBOHYDRATE, 13G TOTAL FAT (2G SATURATED), 9G FIBER, 312MG SODIUM.

PRESSURE COOKER
Indian-Style Lentils

Fresh ginger and cumin give lentils an Indian twist, while diced sweet potatoes add flavor, color, and nutrients.

ACTIVE TIME: 15 MINUTES **TOTAL TIME:** 30 MINUTES **MAKES:** 6 (¾ CUP) SERVINGS

1 onion, chopped

1 tablespoon vegetable oil

1 cup brown lentils, rinsed and picked over

1 large clove garlic, chopped

1½ teaspoons cumin seeds

¼ teaspoon cayenne pepper

1 can (14½ ounces) chicken or vegetable broth or 1¾ cups homemade (pages 17 and 18)

2 tablespoons chopped peeled fresh ginger

1 pound sweet potatoes, peeled and cut into ¾-inch pieces (about 3 cups)

½ teaspoon salt

1 container (8 ounces) plain low-fat yogurt

¼ cup chopped fresh mint or cilantro

1 In Instant Pot® using sauté function, cook onion in oil, uncovered, for 3 minutes, or until softening. Hit cancel to turn off sauté function.

2 Add lentils, garlic, cumin seeds, cayenne, broth, and ¼ cup water. Cover and lock lid. Select Manual/Pressure Cook and cook at high pressure for 7 minutes. Once cooking is complete, release pressure by using a quick release.

3 Add ginger and sweet potatoes on top. Cover and lock lid. Select Manual/Pressure Cook and cook at high pressure for 6 minutes. Once cooking is complete, release pressure by using a quick release. Stir in salt. Transfer to serving bowl.

4 In small bowl, combine yogurt and mint. Serve with lentils.

EACH SERVING: 225 CALORIES, 12G PROTEIN, 38G CARBOHYDRATE, 4G TOTAL FAT (1G SATURATED), 10G FIBER, 329MG SODIUM.

TIP

Lentils, along with other legumes and grains, often require rinsing before cooking. Look for a colander with small openings so these tiny food pieces do not fall through.

SLOW COOKER
Spicy Curry Lentils

These curried lentils are a hearty, healthy meal full of warming spices like cumin and coriander and vegetables including cauliflower. Chopped pistachios as a garnish add crunch. For photo, see page 24.

ACTIVE TIME: 10 MINUTES   **TOTAL TIME:** 8 HOURS, 10 MINUTES   **MAKES:** 6 SERVINGS

2	medium shallots, peeled
1	can (6 ounces) tomato paste
1	jalapeño
4	slices peeled fresh ginger
2	cloves garlic, peeled
2	teaspoons ground cumin
2	teaspoons ground coriander

Salt

Freshly ground black pepper

2	cups Vegetable Broth (page 18)
1½	cups lentils (see Tip)
1	can (15 ounces) light coconut milk
3	cups large cauliflower florets
1	cup frozen peas
1	tablespoon lime juice

Cooked basmati rice, for serving

⅓	cup chopped pistachios, for garnish

1 In food processor, pulse shallots, tomato paste, jalapeño, ginger, garlic, cumin, coriander, and ½ teaspoon each salt and black pepper until mostly smooth; transfer to 7- to 8-quart Instant Pot® bowl.

2 Add broth, lentils, coconut milk, and 1 cup water, stirring to combine. Place cauliflower on top. Cover and set release valve to the venting position. Select Slow Cook and cook on high for 5 hours or on low for 8 hours, or until lentils are tender.

3 Stir in peas, lime juice, and ¼ teaspoon salt. Serve over rice; garnish with pistachios.

EACH SERVING (WITHOUT RICE): ABOUT 320 CALORIES, 19G PROTEIN, 46G CARBOHYDRATE, 8G TOTAL FAT (5G SATURATED), 16G FIBER, 412MG SODIUM.

TIP
Green, black, or brown lentils work nicely in the Instant Pot®. Avoid red lentils as they will fall apart.

PRESSURE COOKER
Risotto Milanese

Saffron-infused Risotto Milanese is delicious as a first course, side, or as a meatless main course when served with a generous mixed salad.

ACTIVE TIME: 10 MINUTES   **TOTAL TIME:** 35 MINUTES   **MAKES:** 6 (1 CUP) SERVINGS

1	medium onion, finely chopped
2	tablespoons butter or olive oil
2	cups Arborio rice or medium-grain rice
½	cup dry white wine
1	can (14½ ounces) chicken broth or 1¾ cups homemade (page 17)
¼	teaspoon loosely packed saffron threads
1	teaspoon salt
½	cup freshly grated Parmesan cheese, plus more for serving

1 In Instant Pot® using sauté function, cook onion in butter, uncovered, for 3 minutes, or until softening. Add rice and stir frequently for 3 minutes, or until grains are opaque. Add wine and cook, stirring, for 1 minute, until absorbed. Hit cancel to turn off sauté function.
2 Stir in broth, saffron, salt, and 1½ cups water. Cover and lock lid. Select Manual/Pressure Cook and cook at high pressure for 6 minutes. Once cooking is complete, release pressure by using a quick release. Let stand 5 minutes, covered. Stir in Parmesan and add additional ¼ cup water if needed. Rice should be tender but firm, and risotto should be creamy. Serve with grated Parmesan.

EACH SERVING: ABOUT 216 CALORIES, 6G PROTEIN, 35G CARBOHYDRATE, 6G TOTAL FAT (3G SATURATED), 3G FIBER, 649MG SODIUM.

Cremini Mushroom Risotto

Prepare Risotto Milanese but in step 1, before adding onion, using sauté function, adjust heat to More and heat **butter**. When hot, add **8 ounces sliced cremini mushrooms** and cook, uncovered, for 5 minutes. Hit cancel, then reselect sauté function (this returns heat to Normal). Add **onion**, and cook as directed. Omit saffron. In step 2, stir in **½ teaspoon chopped fresh thyme** with the **Parmesan**.

EACH SERVING: ABOUT 365 CALORIES, 11G PROTEIN, 64G CARBOHYDRATE, 6G TOTAL FAT (2G SATURATED), 2G FIBER, 635MG SODIUM.

TIP

Arborio rice is a short-grain variety that is used primarily when cooking risottos. Starch is released during the cooking process, resulting in a creamy consistency.

PRESSURE COOKER
Butternut Squash Risotto

With pressure cooking, you can make this impressive
risotto recipe in less than 30 minutes.

ACTIVE TIME: 15 MINUTES   **TOTAL TIME:** 30 MINUTES   **MAKES:** 4 SERVINGS

1	tablespoon olive oil
2	medium shallots, chopped
3	cloves garlic, finely chopped
4	fresh sage leaves, chopped
½	teaspoon salt
2	cups Arborio rice
4	cups lower-sodium chicken or vegetable broth, store-bought or homemade (pages 17 and 18)
1	pound butternut squash, cut into ½-inch pieces
½	cup freshly grated Parmesan cheese
¼	teaspoon ground black pepper

1 In Instant Pot® using sauté function, heat oil and add shallots, garlic, sage, and ¼ teaspoon salt; cook, uncovered, for 2 minutes, stirring. Add rice and cook 2 minutes, stirring. Hit cancel to turn off sauté function.

2 Add broth and butternut squash. Cover and lock lid. Select Manual/Pressure Cook and cook at high pressure for 6 minutes. Once cooking is complete, release pressure by using a quick release.

3 Stir in Parmesan, remaining ¼ teaspoon salt, and pepper. Let stand 5 minutes before serving.

EACH SERVING: ABOUT 465 CALORIES, 11G PROTEIN, 91G CARBOHYDRATE, 7G TOTAL FAT (2G SATURATED), 5G FIBER, 526MG SODIUM.

TIP

You can find peeled butternut squash at your local supermarket. If you are starting with unpeeled squash, you will need 1½ pounds, which is about 3 cups peeled and chopped.

PRESSURE COOKER
Hot Fluffy Rice

For extra-tender rice, use 1¾ cups water. You can easily double the recipe, simply keep the cooking time the same.

ACTIVE TIME: 5 MINUTES **TOTAL TIME:** 20 MINUTES **MAKES:** 4 SERVINGS

1   tablespoon butter, cut into small bits

1   cup regular long-grain rice

½   teaspoon salt

In Instant Pot®, combine butter, rice, salt, and 1½ cups water. Cover and lock lid. Select Manual/Pressure Cook and cook at high pressure for 8 minutes. Once cooking is complete, release pressure by using natural release function. Let stand in cooker 5 minutes. Fluff rice with fork.

EACH SERVING: 210 CALORIES, 4G PROTEIN, 40G CARBOHYDRATE, 3G TOTAL FAT (2G SATURATED), 1G FIBER, 315MG SODIUM.

Brown Rice

Prepare as directed for Hot Fluffy Rice but use **1½ cups water** and **1 cup long-grain brown rice**. Cook at high pressure for 22 minutes. Release pressure by using natural release function.

EACH SERVING: ABOUT 114 CALORIES, 2G PROTEIN, 24G CARBOHYDRATE, 1G TOTAL FAT (0G SATURATED), 3G FIBER, 391MG SODIUM.

TIP

It is not recommended to leave cooked rice in the Keep Warm state for too long as it will affect the texture of the rice.

Fun Flavors

Add these aromatic ingredients
for six delicious variations.

LEMON-PARSLEY RICE

Cook as directed for Hot Fluffy Rice. Stir in **2 tablespoons chopped fresh parsley** and **1 teaspoon freshly grated lemon zest**.

ASIAN RICE

Cook as directed for Hot Fluffy Rice but omit salt. Stir in **2 chopped green onions**, **2 teaspoons soy sauce**, and **¼ teaspoon toasted sesame oil**.

COCONUT RICE

Cook as directed for Hot Fluffy Rice. Stir in **½ cup coconut milk**, **½ teaspoon grated lime zest**, and pinch of **cayenne pepper**.

LEMON-PARMESAN RICE

Cook as directed for Hot Fluffy Rice. Stir in **¼ cup freshly grated Parmesan cheese**, **1 teaspoon grated lemon zest**, and **¼ teaspoon ground black pepper**.

PEPPER JACK RICE

Cook as directed for Hot Fluffy Rice. Stir in **2 ounces shredded (½ cup) Pepper Jack cheese** and **3 thinly sliced green onions**.

GREEN RICE

Cook as directed for Hot Fluffy Rice. Once cooking is complete, release pressure by using a quick release. Stir in **1 package (10 ounces) thawed frozen chopped spinach**. Select sauté and cook at high for 5 minutes, until spinach is heated through. Stir in **2 ounces finely crumbled feta cheese (½ cup)**.

Brown Rice & Vegetable Pilaf

Fragrant herbs and a variety of fresh vegetables complement the nutty flavor of brown rice. Serve this tasty and nutritious dish as a hearty side or a vegetarian main course.

ACTIVE TIME: 10 MINUTES   **TOTAL TIME:** 55 MINUTES   **MAKES:** 6 SERVINGS

8	ounces cremini mushrooms, sliced
1	tablespoon olive or vegetable oil
1	medium onion, chopped
1	stalk celery, chopped
1	cup regular long-grain brown rice
2	carrots, chopped
1	clove garlic, chopped
½	teaspoon dried thyme
¼	teaspoon dried sage
1¼	teaspoons salt
¼	teaspoon ground black pepper

1 In Instant Pot® using sauté function, adjust the heat to More and cook mushrooms in oil, uncovered, for 5 minutes, or until liquid has evaporated. Add onion and celery and cook 3 minutes. Hit cancel to turn off sauté function.

2 Add rice, 1 cup water, carrots, garlic, thyme, sage, salt, and pepper. Cover and lock lid. Select Manual/Pressure Cook and cook at high pressure for 22 minutes. Once cooking is complete, release pressure by using natural release function. Stir to combine.

EACH SERVING: ABOUT 167 CALORIES, 4G PROTEIN, 31G CARBOHYDRATE, 3G TOTAL FAT (0G SATURATED), 3G FIBER, 503MG SODIUM.

PRESSURE COOKER
Basic Bulgur

This grain takes only minutes to prepare when using the pressure-cooking function on your Instant Pot®.

ACTIVE TIME: 5 MINUTES   TOTAL TIME: 30 MINUTES   MAKES: 4 SERVINGS

1   cup coarse or medium-grind bulgur

1   tablespoon canola oil

1½ cups chicken broth, store-bought or homemade (page 17)

¼   teaspoon dried thyme

Pinch of ground nutmeg

In Instant Pot® using sauté function, cook bulgur in oil, uncovered, for 4 minutes, or until fragrantly toasted (nutty). Quickly add broth (all at once); stir in thyme and nutmeg. Cover and lock lid. Select Manual/Pressure Cook and cook at high pressure for 6 minutes. Once cooking is complete, release pressure by using natural release function. Let stand 5 minutes and fluff with fork.

EACH SERVING: ABOUT 133 CALORIES, 5G PROTEIN, 27G CARBOHYDRATE, 1G TOTAL FAT (0G SATURATED), 4G FIBER, 434MG SODIUM.

SLOW COOKER
Steel-Cut Oatmeal

An excellent source of fiber, oatmeal is a tasty, low-fat breakfast. Cook this recipe overnight so you can wake up to an effortless morning meal.

ACTIVE TIME: 5 MINUTES   **TOTAL TIME:** 8 HOURS   **MAKES:** 4 SERVINGS

2   cups low-fat (1%) milk

1½   cups steel-cut oats

¼   teaspoon salt

Spray Instant Pot® bowl with nonstick cooking spray. Add 4 cups water, milk, steel-cut oats, and salt; stir to combine. Cover and set release valve to the venting position. Select Slow Cook and cook on low for 4 hours. Let the oatmeal continue to cook on warm for another 4 hours.

EACH SERVING: ABOUT 280 CALORIES, 12G PROTEIN, 47G CARBOHYDRATE, 5G TOTAL FAT (2G SATURATED), 6G FIBER, 199MG SODIUM.

Blueberry-Almond Oatmeal Topping

In small bowl, mix **1 cup blueberries, ¼ cup chopped toasted almonds**, and **4 teaspoons honey**. Divide topping among servings of oatmeal.

EACH SERVING: ABOUT 95 CALORIES, 3G PROTEIN, 17G CARBOHYDRATE, 2G TOTAL FAT (0G SATURATED), 2G FIBER, 35MG SODIUM.

Apple-Cinnamon Oatmeal Topping

In medium skillet, melt **1 tablespoon butter** over medium-high heat. Add **2 peeled, diced apples**. Reduce heat to medium; cook apples until tender, about 8 minutes, stirring a few times. Stir in **¼ teaspoon ground cinnamon**. Divide apples among servings of oatmeal and sprinkle each bowl with **1 tablespoon brown sugar.**

EACH SERVING: ABOUT 190 CALORIES, 3G PROTEIN, 37G CARBOHYDRATE, 4G TOTAL FAT (2G SATURATED), 3G FIBER, 59MG SODIUM.

Tex-Mex Tortilla Soup
(page 48)

3 Soups, Stews & Chilis

The smell of a simmering soup can immediately draw you into the kitchen. By using the Instant Pot® for slow cooking and pressure cooking, you can develop rich flavors that taste like they have been cooking all day. Unexpected ingredients like a porter in Beer-Braised Beef Stew and chipotles in adobo sauce in Chipotle Lentil Chili lend unique flavors to these nourishing bowls. Classics like Split Pea Soup with Ham and Chunky Chili with Beans are perfect for any chilly night. Slowly cooked to perfection or pressurized to quickly develop robust flavors, these recipes are great additions to the weeknight meal rotation.

PRESSURE COOKER
Winter Root Vegetable Soup

A medley of root vegetables—including celery root, parsnips, turnips, and carrots—lends a delightful sweetness to this dish. Top this hearty soup with a dollop of sour cream and a sprinkling of chives.

ACTIVE TIME: 30 MINUTES   **TOTAL TIME:** 45 MINUTES   **MAKES:** 8 SERVINGS

2   tablespoons olive oil

1   large onion, chopped (1½ cups)

6   cloves garlic, finely chopped

6   cups chicken broth, store-bought or homemade (page 17)

2   tablespoons apple cider vinegar

1   pound celery root, peeled and cut into 1½-inch chunks

1   large baking potato (12 ounces), peeled and cut into 1½-inch chunks

1   large sweet potato (12 ounces), peeled and cut into 1½-inch chunks

2   parsnips, peeled and cut into 1½-inch chunks

2   large carrots (8 ounces each), peeled and cut into 1 ½-inch chunks

1   turnip (4 ounces), peeled and cut into 1½-inch chunks

1   teaspoon finely chopped peeled fresh ginger

½   teaspoon salt

¼   teaspoon ground cumin

¼   teaspoon curry powder

¼   teaspoon ground cinnamon

⅛   teaspoon cayenne pepper

1 In Instant Pot® using sauté function, heat oil. Add onion and cook, uncovered, for 3 minutes, or until softened, stirring occasionally. Add garlic and cook 1 minute, stirring. Hit cancel to turn off sauté function.

2 Add broth, vinegar, vegetables, ginger, salt, and spices. Cover and lock lid. Select Manual/ Pressure Cook and cook at high pressure for 8 minutes. Once cooking is complete, release pressure by using a quick release.

3 Transfer soup in batches to blender or food processor and blend until smooth.

EACH SERVING: ABOUT 215 CALORIES, 7G PROTEIN, 39G CARBOHYDRATE, 4G TOTAL FAT (1G SATURATED), 7G FIBER, 290MG SODIUM.

TIP

Cooking the vegetables together under pressure until they are soft allows you to easily puree them into a creamy, smooth consistency.

Tex-Mex Tortilla Soup

Homemade crispy tortilla strips give this hearty chicken soup
a healthy crunch. For photo, see page 44.

ACTIVE TIME: 20 MINUTES   **TOTAL TIME:** 5 HOURS, 20 MINUTES   **MAKES:** 6 SERVINGS

2½ pounds bone-in, skin-on chicken thighs, skin removed

4 cups lower-sodium chicken broth, store-bought or homemade (page 17)

3 large stalks celery, sliced

3 medium carrots, sliced

2 poblano peppers, seeded and chopped

1 medium onion, chopped

3 cloves garlic, chopped

1 tablespoon ground cumin

1 tablespoon ground coriander

2 cans (15 ounces each) cannellini (white kidney beans), rinsed and drained

Salt

8 ounces Monterey Jack cheese, shredded

2 tablespoons lime juice

Chopped avocado, for serving

Cilantro leaves, for serving

Sour cream, for serving

Baked Tortilla Strips, for serving (optional)

1 In Instant Pot®, combine chicken, broth, celery, carrots, poblanos, onion, garlic, cumin, coriander, beans, and ½ teaspoon salt. Cover and set release valve to the venting position. Select Slow Cook and cook on low for 4 to 5 hours, or until carrots are tender.

2 Remove and discard bones from chicken; shred chicken and return meat to Instant Pot®.

3 Add cheese, lime juice, and ¼ teaspoon salt, stirring until cheese melts. Serve the soup in individual bowls topped with avocado, cilantro, sour cream, and, if desired, Baked Tortilla Strips.

EACH SERVING (WITHOUT TORTILLA STRIPS): ABOUT 445 CALORIES, 40G PROTEIN, 34G CARBOHYDRATE, 16G FAT (7G SATURATED), 14G FIBER, 1,070MG SODIUM.

Baked Tortilla Strips

Preheat oven to 425°F. Stack **4 corn tortillas**; thinly slice into ⅛-inch-wide strips. Arrange in single layer on large baking sheet. Spray all over with **nonstick cooking spray**. Bake 4 to 5 minutes, or until deep golden brown. Let cool completely.

TIP

You can proceed with recipe through step 2 and then hold on the Instant Pot®'s warm setting for up to 3 hours.

PRESSURE COOKER
Split Pea Soup with Ham

This hearty old-fashioned favorite is chock-full of veggies
and has a nice smoky flavor from the ham hocks.

ACTIVE TIME: 10 MINUTES   **TOTAL TIME:** 55 MINUTES   **MAKES:** 3 (SCANT 2 CUP) SERVINGS

1 tablespoon vegetable oil

1 white turnip (6 ounces), peeled and chopped (optional)

1 carrot, chopped

1 stalk celery, chopped

1 medium onion, finely chopped

1¼ cups (8 ounces) split peas, rinsed and picked over

2 smoked ham hocks (1½ pounds total)

1 bay leaf

¼ teaspoon ground allspice

¾ teaspoon salt

¼ teaspoon ground black pepper

1 In Instant Pot®, combine oil, turnip (if using), carrot, celery, onion, split peas, ham hocks, 4 cups water, bay leaf, allspice, salt, and pepper. Cover and lock lid. Select Manual/Pressure Cook and cook at high pressure for 8 minutes. Once cooking is complete, release pressure by using natural release function.

2 Discard bay leaf. Transfer ham hocks to cutting board; discard skin and bones. Finely chop any meat. Stir into soup.

EACH SERVING: ABOUT 455 CALORIES, 29G PROTEIN, 54G CARBOHYDRATE, 14G TOTAL FAT (4G SATURATED), 21G FIBER, 752MG SODIUM.

German Lentil Soup

Prepare as above, but omit turnip. Substitute **8 ounces lentils**, rinsed and picked over, for split peas, and substitute ½ **teaspoon thyme** for allspice.

EACH SERVING: ABOUT 445 CALORIES, 31G PROTEIN, 50G CARBOHYDRATE, 14G TOTAL FAT (4G SATURATED), 19G FIBER, 745MG SODIUM.

SLOW COOKER
Smoky Vegan Black Bean Soup

Vegetables are the true stars of this nutritious soup, making it a perfect option for your plant-focused friends.

ACTIVE TIME: 20 MINUTES   TOTAL TIME: 6 HOURS, 20 MINUTES   MAKES: 6 SERVINGS

2   tablespoons olive oil

2   medium carrots, chopped

2   stalks celery, sliced

1   medium onion, finely chopped

¼   cup tomato paste

3   cloves garlic, crushed with garlic press

1½ teaspoons ground cumin

3   cups lower-sodium vegetable or chicken broth, store-bought or homemade (pages 18 and 17)

3   cans (15 ounces each) lower-sodium black beans, undrained

1   cup frozen corn kernels

Avocado chunks and cilantro leaves, for serving

1 In Instant Pot® using sauté function, heat oil. Add carrots, celery, and onion. Cook, uncovered, for 6 to 8 minutes, or until starting to brown, stirring occasionally. Add tomato paste, garlic, and cumin. Cook, stirring, 1 to 2 minutes, or until garlic is golden and tomato paste has browned. Stir in ½ cup broth, scraping up any browned bits.

2 Add beans, corn, and remaining 2½ cups broth to pot. Cover and set release valve to the venting position. Select Slow Cook and cook on high for 4 hours or low for 6 hours. Serve with avocado and cilantro.

EACH SERVING: ABOUT 325 CALORIES, 14G PROTEIN, 51G CARBOHYDRATES, 11G FAT (1G SATURATED), 19G FIBER, 535MG SODIUM.

TIP
Dried beans do not work well for this dish. Acidic ingredients, such as the tomato paste, make the beans stay tough. They will take longer to cook.

SLOW COOKER
Kielbasa Stew

A protein-rich stew featuring Polish sausage and lentils
packs lots of cholesterol-lowering fiber.

ACTIVE TIME: 20 MINUTES   **TOTAL TIME:** 10 HOURS, 20 MINUTES   **MAKES:** 6 SERVINGS

2   teaspoons vegetable oil

1   small yellow onion, sliced

2   stalks celery, sliced

1   teaspoon caraway seeds

3   bay leaves

Salt

1   pound Yukon Gold potatoes, scrubbed
    and cut into 1-inch chunks

2   cups lentils

4   cups lower-sodium chicken broth,
    store-bought or homemade (page 17)

1   cup apple cider

14 ounces kielbasa, thinly sliced

1   cup sauerkraut, drained

Grainy mustard, for serving (optional)

Chopped parsley, for garnish (optional)

1 In Instant Pot® using sauté function, heat oil.
Add onion, celery, caraway seeds, bay leaves,
and ¼ teaspoon salt. Cook, uncovered, for 1 to
3 minutes, or until slightly softened, stirring
frequently.

2 Add potatoes, lentils, chicken broth, cider, and
kielbasa to pot. Cover and set release valve to the
venting position. Select Slow Cook and cook on
high for 6 hours or low for 9 to 10 hours.

3 Discard bay leaves. Stir in sauerkraut. If
desired, serve with grainy mustard and garnish
with parsley.

EACH SERVING: ABOUT 430 CALORIES, 30G PROTEIN,
67G CARBOHYDRATE, 5G TOTAL FAT (1G SATURATED),
17G FIBER, 895MG SODIUM.

SLOW COOKER
Spiced Chickpea Stew

Add a fried or poached egg to the top of this stew for a jolt of extra protein. Plus, the broken yolk adds richness to the stew.

ACTIVE TIME: 15 MINUTES   **TOTAL TIME:** 5 HOURS, 25 MINUTES   **MAKES:** 4 SERVINGS

1¼ pounds Yukon Gold potatoes, cut into 1-inch chunks

3 medium carrots, peeled and chopped

1 can (15 ounces) chickpeas, drained

1 pound zucchini, cut into 1-inch chunks

2 teaspoons fennel seeds

1 teaspoon ground coriander

1 teaspoon salt

½ teaspoon ground cinnamon

½ teaspoon ground black pepper

1 lemon, quartered

1 cup frozen peas

4 large eggs, fried or poached

Chopped fresh mint, for garnish

1 In Instant Pot®, layer potatoes, carrots, chickpeas, and zucchini.

2 In bowl, whisk together 1 cup water, fennel seeds, coriander, salt, cinnamon, and pepper and pour over vegetables. Top with lemon quarters. Cover and set release valve to the venting position. Select Slow Cook and cook on high for 5 hours; 10 minutes before serving, add frozen peas to cooker and re-cover.

3 To serve, remove and discard lemon. Divide among 4 bowls. Top each with 1 fried or poached egg and garnish with mint.

EACH SERVING: ABOUT 365 CALORIES, 19G PROTEIN, 56G CARBOHYDRATE, 7G TOTAL FAT (2G SATURATED), 7G FIBER, 940MG SODIUM.

Beer-Braised Beef Stew

Use a dark beer like stout, porter, or brown ale to deliver
the heartiness needed to match beef's flavor.

ACTIVE TIME: 30 MINUTES   **TOTAL TIME:** 10 HOURS, 30 MINUTES   **MAKES:** 8 SERVINGS

1   boneless beef chuck roast (about 4 pounds)

Salt

Freshly ground black pepper

2   tablespoons vegetable oil

2   medium onions, sliced

2   pounds carrots, peeled and sliced

1   bottle (12 ounces) dark beer (such as a brown ale)

⅓   cup distilled white vinegar

½   cup ketchup

⅓   cup golden raisins

3   tablespoons brown sugar

Green beans, for serving (optional)

1   Rub roast with ½ teaspoon each salt and pepper. In Instant Pot® using sauté function, heat vegetable oil until very hot. Brown roast on all sides. Transfer to a plate.

2   To pot, still on sauté function, add onions, carrots, ¼ teaspoon salt, and 2 tablespoons water and cook, uncovered, 2 to 4 minutes, or until slightly softened, stirring. Add beer and vinegar. Simmer 4 minutes, stirring. Hit cancel to turn off sauté function.

3   Add ketchup, raisins, and brown sugar to pot. Cover and set release valve to the venting position. Select Slow Cook and cook on low for 10 hours, or until tender.

4   Skim and discard fat from cooking liquid. Slice meat and serve with vegetables; drizzle with cooking liquids. If desired, serve green beans alongside.

EACH SERVING: ABOUT 580 CALORIES, 48G PROTEIN, 28G CARBOHYDRATE, 30G TOTAL FAT (12G SATURATED), 4G FIBER, 535G SODIUM.

Southwestern Chicken Stew

Infuse your winter stew with the personality of the Southwest: bright, rich flavors and a subtle spice.

ACTIVE TIME: 15 MINUTES **TOTAL TIME:** 4 HOURS, 30 MINUTES **MAKES:** 8 SERVINGS

1   can (28 ounces) fire-roasted tomatoes

2   green onions, trimmed and cut into thirds, plus 2 green onions, thinly sliced, for serving

2   chipotle chiles in adobo sauce

2   tablespoons adobo sauce

2   cloves garlic

2   teaspoons chili powder

1   teaspoon ground cumin

Salt

1¼   pounds boneless, skinless chicken breasts

2   cups chicken broth, store-bought or homemade (page 17)

1 pound thin spaghetti, broken into thirds (see Tip)

1½   cups finely shredded Monterey Jack cheese, for serving

Chopped fresh cilantro, for serving

1 In blender, puree tomatoes, green onions, chipotles, adobo sauce, garlic, chili powder, cumin, and 1 teaspoon salt until smooth.

2 Transfer contents of blender to Instant Pot®. Arrange chicken on top (do not submerge). Cover and set release valve to the venting position. Select Slow Cook and cook on low for 3½ hours, or until chicken is cooked (165°F). Transfer chicken to cutting board.

3 In measuring cup, combine broth, ½ cup water, and ¼ teaspoon salt. Microwave on high 1 minute. Add broth mixture to pot. Add spaghetti, pushing down to fully submerge. Re-cover and cook on low 30 to 45 minutes, testing after 30 minutes, or until pasta is al dente and most of liquid has been absorbed, stirring once.

4 While pasta cooks, pull chicken into chunks.

5 Once pasta is cooked, return chicken to pot, tossing to combine. To serve, top with shredded cheese, sliced green onions, and cilantro.

EACH SERVING: ABOUT 410 CALORIES, 29G PROTEIN, 50G CARBOHYDRATE, 10G FAT (4G SATURATED), 4G FIBER, 1,120MG SODIUM.

TIP

Make sure to use "thin spaghetti"—not angel hair or spaghettini; each of those is too thin and will get overcooked and mushy.

PRESSURE COOKER
Winter Squash & Lentil Stew

A bowl of this stew warms chilly fingers and toes with seasonal flavors of sweet butternut squash and savory lentils. Seconds, anyone?

ACTIVE TIME: 15 MINUTES   **TOTAL TIME:** 35 MINUTES   **MAKES:** 6 SERVINGS

2   medium shallots, thinly sliced

1   tablespoon finely chopped peeled fresh ginger

1   tablespoon vegetable oil

1   teaspoon ground coriander

½   teaspoon ground cardamom

1   small butternut squash, peeled, seeded, and cut into 1½-inch chunks

1   pound green lentils, rinsed and picked over

6   cups chicken or vegetable broth, store-bought or homemade (pages 17 and 18)

Salt

5   cups packed baby spinach

1   tablespoon apple cider vinegar

Freshly ground black pepper

1 In Instant Pot® using sauté function, cook shallots and ginger in oil, uncovered, for 5 minutes, or until shallots are golden, stirring. Add coriander and cardamom; cook 1 minute, stirring. Hit cancel to turn off sauté function.

2 Add squash, lentils, broth, and ¼ teaspoon salt to pot. Cover and lock lid. Select Manual/Pressure Cook and cook at high pressure for 12 minutes. Once cooking is complete, release pressure by using a quick release.

3 Stir in spinach, vinegar, and ½ teaspoon each of salt and pepper.

EACH SERVING: ABOUT 325 CALORIES, 19G PROTEIN, 57G CARBOHYDRATE, 4G FAT (0G SATURATED), 15G FIBER, 705MG SODIUM.

Chipotle Lentil Chili

Serve this chili topped with avocadoes, cilantro,
and cheese as a great appetizer on game day.

ACTIVE TIME: 15 MINUTES   **TOTAL TIME:** 35 MINUTES   **MAKES:** 6 SERVINGS

1   medium onion, coarsely chopped

1   medium green bell pepper, coarsely
chopped

1   tablespoon canola oil

2   large cloves garlic, chopped

3   tablespoons mild chili powder

1   can (28 ounces) diced tomatoes

2   cans (14½ ounces each) lower-sodium
vegetable broth or 4 cups homemade
(page 18) plus ½ cup water

2   cups brown lentils, rinsed and picked over

1   to 2 chipotles in adobo sauce, seeded
and chopped

½   cup sun-dried tomatoes (about 10 halves),
chopped

1   teaspoon ground cumin

½   teaspoon salt

Diced avocado, shredded Cheddar cheese,
chopped fresh cilantro, sour cream, and
lime wedges, for serving

1 In Instant Pot® using sauté function, cook onion and bell pepper in oil, uncovered, for 3 minutes, or until softening. Stir in garlic and 2 tablespoons chili powder and cook 1 minute. Hit cancel to turn off sauté function.

2 Stir in tomatoes, broth, lentils, chipotles, and sun-dried tomatoes. Cover and lock lid. Select Manual/Pressure Cook and cook at high pressure for 12 minutes. Once cooking is complete, release pressure by using a quick release. Stir in cumin, salt, and remaining 1 tablespoon chili powder. Cover and keep warm for 10 minutes, until thickened slightly and flavored through.

3 Serve with avocado, Cheddar, cilantro, sour cream, and lime wedges.

EACH SERVING: ABOUT 315 CALORIES, 19G PROTEIN, 53G CARBOHYDRATE, 4G TOTAL FAT (0G SATURATED), 18G FIBER, 932MG SODIUM.

SLOW COOKER
Cincinnati Chili

Tailor the recipe to your pantry and taste—
use whichever beans you have on the shelf.

ACTIVE TIME: 5 MINUTES **TOTAL TIME:** 6 HOURS, 5 MINUTES **MAKES:** 6 SERVINGS

1½ pounds ground beef

1   can (15 ounces) kidney beans, rinsed
and drained

1   can (15 ounces) tomato sauce

1   medium onion, chopped

2   tablespoons brown sugar

2   tablespoons unsweetened cocoa

2   teaspoons chipotle chile powder

2   teaspoons ground cumin

1½ teaspoons ground cinnamon

Salt

Freshly ground black pepper

1 pound cooked spaghetti, for serving

4 ounces sharp Cheddar cheese, shredded

4 green onions, thinly sliced

1 In Instant Pot®, combine beef, beans, tomato
sauce, onion, brown sugar, cocoa, chipotle
powder, cumin, cinnamon, and ½ teaspoon each
salt and black pepper; stir together, breaking up
ground beef. Cover and set release valve to the
venting position. Select Slow Cook and cook on
low for 6 hours.

2 When ready to serve, spoon over spaghetti.
Top with Cheddar and green onions.

EACH SERVING (WITHOUT SPAGHETTI): ABOUT
655 CALORIES, 44G PROTEIN, 81G CARBOHYDRATE,
17G TOTAL FAT (8G SATURATED), 10G FIBER,
885MG SODIUM.

TIP

This dish is equally delish over tortilla
chips, in baked potatoes, or just by itself
in a bowl.

Chunky Chili with Beans

When purchasing chili powder, check the
ingredients to find a sodium-free blend.

ACTIVE TIME: 40 MINUTES **TOTAL TIME:** 10 HOURS, 40 MINUTES **MAKES:** ABOUT 10 (1¼ CUP) SERVINGS

4   slices bacon, cut crosswise into ½-inch pieces

1½ pounds boneless pork shoulder, trimmed of excess fat and cut into 1-inch chunks

1½ pounds boneless beef chuck, trimmed and cut into 1-inch chunks

1   jumbo onion (about 1 pound), coarsely chopped

¼   cup chili powder

4   large cloves garlic, crushed with garlic press

1   tablespoon ground cumin

1½ teaspoons dried oregano

½   teaspoon salt

1   can (28 ounces) diced tomatoes

3   cans (15 to 19 ounces each) pinto beans, rinsed and drained

Sour cream, for serving (optional)

1 In Instant Pot® using sauté function, cook bacon, uncovered, until browned and crisp, stirring occasionally. With slotted spoon, transfer bacon to plate; cover and refrigerate until ready to use. Pour bacon fat into cup and reserve.

2 Choose sauté again and adjust heat to More. Add pork and beef in 3 batches and cook until well browned. As it browns, transfer meat with slotted spoon to plate.

3 Hit cancel, then reselect sauté function (this returns heat to Normal). Return 1 tablespoon bacon fat to pot, add onion, and cook, uncovered, 8 to 10 minutes, or until tender, stirring occasionally. Stir in chili powder, garlic, cumin, oregano, and salt; cook 30 seconds to toast spices. Add tomatoes and 1 cup water, stirring to scrape up browned bits from bottom of pot. Hit cancel to turn off sauté function.

4 Add beans to pot; stir well to combine. Cover and set release valve to the venting position. Select Slow Cook and cook on high for 4 to 5 hours or low for 8 to 10 hours, or until meat is fork-tender. Skim and discard any fat from chili. Stir in bacon. Serve with sour cream, if desired.

EACH SERVING: ABOUT 400 CALORIES, 39G PROTEIN, 31G CARBOHYDRATE, 13G TOTAL FAT (4G SATURATED), 10G FIBER, 875MG SODIUM.

Latin Chicken with Black Beans &
Sweet Potatoes (page 78)

4 | Chicken

Chicken is versatile and has been used in dishes all over the world. Moist-heat techniques like braising are associated with tough cuts of meat, but chicken can also benefit from this cooking method. Skip the rotisserie chicken at the grocery store and make Chicken with Walnut-Herb Sauce using the slow cooker function. We suggest you save leftovers for weekday lunches. Stewed in tomatoes with rich spices like coriander, cumin, and cinnamon, Chicken Tagine is tender to the bone. Plus, classics like Chicken Fricassee and Quicker Coq au Vin Blanc use the pressure-cooking function to build intensified flavor.

SLOW COOKER
Sesame Garlic Chicken

This healthier take on a Chinese favorite is almost as easy as ordering in.

ACTIVE TIME: 20 MINUTES **TOTAL TIME:** 6 HOURS, 20 MINUTES **MAKES:** 6 SERVINGS

⅓ cup mirin (sweet rice wine)

⅓ cup soy sauce

⅓ cup toasted sesame oil

1 tablespoon brown sugar

2 pounds boneless, skinless chicken breasts

8 cloves garlic

1 (1-inch) piece fresh ginger, sliced into thin slices

4 cups cooked white rice, for serving

1 pound broccoli florets, steamed, for serving

Sliced green onions and red chiles, for garnish

1 In small bowl, whisk together mirin, soy sauce, sesame oil, and brown sugar. In Instant Pot®, layer chicken breasts, soy mixture, garlic, and fresh ginger. Cover and set release valve to the venting position. Select Slow Cook and cook on low for 5 to 6 hours, until chicken is tender.

2 Transfer chicken to cutting board; shred and return to pot. Serve chicken mixture with white rice and broccoli florets. Garnish with green onions and chiles.

EACH SERVING: ABOUT 475 CALORIES, 40G PROTEIN, 41G CARBOHYDRATE, 17G TOTAL FAT (3G SATURATED), 3G FIBER, 978MG SODIUM.

SLOW COOKER
Chicken Tagine

This Moroccan stew features tender chicken and butternut squash whose flavors have melded with garlic, onion, and rich spices in the gentle heat of the slow cooker function.

ACTIVE TIME: 20 MINUTES   **TOTAL TIME:** 8 HOURS, 20 MINUTES   **MAKES:** 6 SERVINGS

1   medium butternut squash

2   medium tomatoes

1   medium onion

2   cloves garlic

1   can (15 to 19 ounces) chickpeas, rinsed and drained

1   cup chicken broth, store-bought or homemade (page 17)

⅓   cup raisins

2   teaspoons ground coriander

2   teaspoons ground cumin

½   teaspoon ground cinnamon

½   teaspoon salt

¼   teaspoon ground black pepper

3   pounds bone-in, skinless chicken thighs

1   box (10 ounces) plain couscous

½   cup pitted green olives

1 In Instant Pot®, combine squash, tomatoes, onion, garlic, chickpeas, broth, and raisins. In cup, combine coriander, cumin, cinnamon, salt, and black pepper. Rub spice mixture all over chicken thighs; place chicken on top of vegetable mixture. Cover and set release valve to the venting position. Select Slow Cook and cook on high for 4 hours or low for 8 hours.

2 About 10 minutes before serving, prepare couscous according to package directions.

3 To serve, fluff couscous with fork. Stir olives into chicken mixture. Serve chicken mixture over couscous.

EACH SERVING: ABOUT 545 CALORIES, 39G PROTEIN, 80G CARBOHYDRATE, 9G TOTAL FAT (2G SATURATED), 10G FIBER, 855MG SODIUM.

TIP

Did you know that 40 percent of the fat in chicken comes from the skin? That's why we got rid of it in this dish!

PRESSURE COOKER
Chicken Cacciatore

This tender chicken leg is completely infused
with Italian herbs and flavors.

ACTIVE TIME: 10 MINUTES   **TOTAL TIME:** 35 MINUTES   **MAKES:** 4 SERVINGS

1   package (8 ounces) sliced cremini
    mushrooms

1   tablespoon olive oil

1   medium onion, thinly sliced

3   cloves garlic, thinly sliced

2   tablespoons all-purpose flour

1   can (28 ounces) diced tomatoes

1¼ teaspoons dried oregano

¼   teaspoon salt

¼   teaspoon crushed red pepper flakes

4   bone-in, skinless chicken thighs
    (about 8 ounces each)

1   medium yellow or green bell pepper,
    thinly sliced

3   tablespoons chopped fresh basil or parsley

1   teaspoon balsamic vinegar

Freshly grated Parmesan cheese, for serving

1 In Instant Pot® select sauté function and adjust heat to More. Cook mushrooms in oil, uncovered, for 4 minutes. Stir in onion and garlic; cook 4 minutes, or until onions soften. Sprinkle on flour and stir. Add tomatoes, oregano, salt, and pepper flakes. Stir and scrape up any browned bits on pan bottom.

2 Add chicken thighs, pressing into sauce. Cover and lock lid. Select Manual/Pressure Cook and cook at high pressure for 9 minutes. Once cooking is complete, release pressure by using a quick release. Transfer chicken to plate. Stir and scrape any bits off bottom of pan if needed.

3 Choose sauté function and adjust heat to More. Stir in bell pepper and cook 4 minutes, or until peppers are just tender. Stir in basil and balsamic vinegar. Serve with grated Parmesan.

EACH SERVING: ABOUT 295 CALORIES, 31G PROTEIN, 21G CARBOHYDRATE, 9G TOTAL FAT (2G SATURATED), 3G FIBER, 724MG SODIUM.

TIP

This dish is great served over creamy
polenta.

SLOW COOKER
Moroccan-Spiced Chicken

Pumpkin pie spice is a blend of cinnamon, ginger, nutmeg, allspice, and cloves: a shortcut for lots of warm spices in a single scoop.

ACTIVE TIME: 25 MINUTES **TOTAL TIME:** 5 HOURS, 25 MINUTES, PLUS MARINATING **MAKES:** 6 SERVINGS

2½ pounds bone-in, skinless chicken thighs

1 teaspoon ground cumin

½ teaspoon ground coriander

½ teaspoon pumpkin pie spice

½ teaspoon ground black pepper

¾ teaspoon salt

1½ cups chicken broth, store-bought or homemade (page 17)

1 can (15 ounces) diced fire-roasted tomatoes

1 can (15 ounces) cannellini (white kidney beans), rinsed and drained

1 large sweet potato, peeled and chopped

1 medium onion, chopped

½ cup dried apricots, sliced

Sliced almonds, for garnish

1 In gallon-size resealable plastic bag, combine chicken thighs, cumin, coriander, pumpkin pie spice, pepper, and ½ teaspoon salt; refrigerate overnight.

2 In Instant Pot®, combine chicken broth, tomatoes, beans, sweet potato, onion, and apricots. Place chicken in pot on top of vegetables. Cover and set release valve to the venting position. Select Slow Cook and cook on low for 5 hours, or until chicken is cooked through (165°F).

3 Transfer chicken to cutting board. Skim and discard fat from cooking liquid. Stir remaining ¼ teaspoon salt into cooking liquid.

4 Serve chicken and vegetables drizzled with cooking liquid and garnished with sliced almonds.

EACH SERVING: ABOUT 340 CALORIES, 31G PROTEIN, 28G CARBOHYDRATE, 11G TOTAL FAT (3G SATURATED), 5G FIBER, 750MG SODIUM.

TIP

Serve this chicken dish with couscous on the side.

Thai Chicken & Noodles

Red curry and coconut milk add a richness
to this Southeast Asia-inspired dinner.

ACTIVE TIME: 25 MINUTES   **TOTAL TIME:** 5 HOURS, 25 MINUTES, PLUS MARINATING   **MAKES:** 8 SERVINGS

2½ pounds bone-in, skinless chicken thighs

1   tablespoon Thai red curry paste, plus
    2 tablespoons

½   teaspoon grated lime zest

½   teaspoon ground black pepper

¾   teaspoon salt

1   can (15 ounces) coconut milk

¼   cup peanut butter

2   tablespoons lower-sodium soy sauce

1   pound green beans, trimmed and cut into
    1-inch lengths

1   large shallot, chopped

8   ounces cooked rice noodles

Chopped unsalted roasted peanuts

Fresh cilantro, for garnish

Lime wedges, for serving

1 In gallon-size resealable plastic bag, combine
chicken thighs, 1 tablespoon curry paste, lime
zest, pepper, and ½ teaspoon salt; refrigerate
overnight.

2 In Instant Pot®, combine coconut milk,
peanut butter, soy sauce, green beans, shallot,
and remaining 2 tablespoons curry paste. Place
chicken in pot on top of vegetables. Cover and
set release valve to the venting position. Select
Slow Cook and cook on low for 5 hours, or until
chicken is cooked through (165°F).

3 Transfer chicken to cutting board. Skim and
discard fat from cooking liquid. Stir remaining
¼ teaspoon salt into cooking liquid. Pull meat
from bones (discard fat, bones, and gristle);
return to pot. Toss with cooked rice noodles.

4 Serve with chopped peanuts, cilantro, and
lime wedges.

EACH SERVING: ABOUT 445 CALORIES, 25G PROTEIN,
35G CARBOHYDRATE, 23G TOTAL FAT (12G SATURATED),
3G FIBER, 600MG SODIUM.

Latin Chicken with Black Beans & Sweet Potatoes

This spicy, smoky dish provides a good portion of your daily fiber, thanks to the beans, as well as a whopping amount of beta-carotene from the sweet potatoes. For photo, see page 68.

ACTIVE TIME: 15 MINUTES **TOTAL TIME:** 8 HOURS, 15 MINUTES **MAKES:** 6 SERVINGS

3   pounds bone-in, skinless chicken thighs

2   teaspoons ground cumin

Salt

Freshly ground black pepper

1   teaspoon smoked paprika or ½ teaspoon chopped chipotle chiles in adobo sauce

½   teaspoon ground allspice

1   cup chicken broth, store-bought or homemade (page 17)

½   cup salsa

3   cloves garlic, crushed with garlic press

2   cans (15 ounces each) black beans, rinsed and drained

2   pounds sweet potatoes, peeled and cut into 2-inch chunks

1   cup roasted red peppers, cut into strips

⅓   cup loosely packed fresh cilantro leaves, chopped

Lime wedges, for serving

1   Sprinkle chicken thighs with ½ teaspoon ground cumin, ¼ teaspoon salt, and ¼ teaspoon black pepper. In Instant Pot®, using sauté function on high, cook chicken thighs for 10 minutes, or until well browned on all sides. Remove chicken to a plate.

2   In Instant Pot®, combine smoked paprika, allspice, chicken broth, salsa, garlic, and remaining 1½ teaspoons cumin, along with the beans and sweet potatoes.

3   Place chicken on top of potato mixture and spoon some of the liquids over the chicken. Cover and set release valve to the venting position. Select Slow Cook and cook on high for 4 hours or low for 8 hours, or until the chicken is cooked through (165°F).

4   Remove chicken pieces to large platter. Gently stir roasted red pepper strips into potato mixture. Spoon mixture over chicken. Sprinkle with cilantro and serve with lime wedges.

EACH SERVING: ABOUT 415 CALORIES, 36G PROTEIN, 61G CARBOHYDRATE, 6G TOTAL FAT (1G SATURATED), 12G FIBER, 875MG SODIUM.

PRESSURE COOKER
Chicken Fricassee

A dash of lemon zest in the marinade adds a citrusy brightness to this classic chicken dinner featuring mushrooms, peas, and potatoes.

ACTIVE TIME: 15 MINUTES **TOTAL TIME:** 55 MINUTES **MAKES:** 6 SERVINGS

6   large bone-in, skinless chicken thighs (2½ pounds total)

1   teaspoon salt

½   teaspoon ground black pepper

2   tablespoons butter

2   leeks, white and pale green parts only, halved lengthwise, sliced, and rinsed well

3   cloves garlic, crushed with garlic press

1   teaspoon herbes de Provence

8   ounces white mushrooms, sliced

1½ pounds medium red potatoes, halved

1   cup chicken broth, store-bought or homemade (page 17)

1½ cups frozen peas

⅔   cup light sour cream

1   tablespoon all-purpose flour

Chopped fresh parsley, for garnish

1 Season chicken with ¾ teaspoon salt and ¼ teaspoon pepper.

2 In Instant Pot® using sauté function, melt 1 tablespoon butter. Add chicken to pot in batches; cook 5 minutes per side, or until browned. Transfer chicken to plate.

3 To pot, add leeks and garlic; cook 2 minutes, stirring. Return chicken to pot. Sprinkle with herbes de Provence. Top with mushrooms and potatoes; add broth. Cover and lock lid. Select Manual/Pressure Cook and cook at high pressure for 12 minutes. Once cooking is complete, release pressure by using a quick release.

4 Transfer potatoes to large bowl and cover with foil to keep hot. Remove chicken to plate. Add peas to pot and select sauté function. In small bowl, whisk 1/3 cup sour cream and flour until smooth. Once liquid in pot is boiling, stir in sour cream mixture. Simmer 2 minutes, or until thickened. Return chicken to pot.

5 Meanwhile, coarsely mash potatoes. Add remaining 1 tablespoon butter, 1/3 cup sour cream, ¼ teaspoon salt, and ¼ teaspoon pepper to potatoes; mash. Serve chicken over potatoes and sprinkle with parsley.

EACH SERVING: 355 CALORIES, 30G PROTEIN, 33G CARBOHYDRATE, 12G TOTAL FAT (6G SATURATED), 5G FIBER, 586MG SODIUM.

TIP

Serve with your favorite white wine for an impressive at-home dinner date.

PRESSURE COOKER
No-Time Tikka Masala

This Indian favorite is on the table in under an hour.

ACTIVE TIME: 15 MINUTES **TOTAL TIME:** 35 MINUTES **MAKES:** 4 SERVINGS

1   tablespoon vegetable oil

1   medium onion, finely chopped

1   tablespoon grated peeled fresh ginger

3   cloves garlic, crushed with garlic press

1   tablespoon curry powder

1   teaspoon paprika

1½   pounds boneless, skinless chicken thighs, cut into 1 ½-inch chunks

1   cup canned crushed tomatoes

½   cup chicken broth, store-bought or homemade (page 17)

2   teaspoons sugar

¾   teaspoon salt

½   cup half-and-half

1½   teaspoons cornstarch

¼   cup cilantro leaves, chopped

Hot Fluffy Rice (page 38), for serving

1 In Instant Pot® using sauté function, heat oil. Add onion and cook, uncovered, for 4 minutes, or until golden, stirring occasionally. Add ginger and garlic; cook 1 minute, stirring. Add curry powder and paprika; cook 30 seconds, stirring. Stir in chicken, tomatoes, broth, sugar, and salt. Hit cancel to turn off sauté function.

2 Cover and lock lid. Select Manual/Pressure Cook and cook at high pressure for 12 minutes. Once cooking is complete, release pressure by using a quick release.

3 In cup, mix half-and-half and cornstarch. Set pot to sauté function and bring chicken to a simmer. Stir in half-and-half mixture. Simmer 2 minutes, or until thickened, stirring occasionally. Stir in cilantro. Serve with Hot Fluffy Rice.

EACH SERVING (WITHOUT RICE): 335 CALORIES, 37G PROTEIN, 14G CARBOHYDRATE, 14G TOTAL FAT (4G SATURATED), 3G FIBER, 738MG SODIUM.

SLOW COOKER
Caribbean Chicken Thighs

Topped with a salsa of sweet mango, creamy avocado, and spicy jalapeños, this chicken recipe has serious island flair.

ACTIVE TIME: 10 MINUTES   **TOTAL TIME:** 8 HOURS, 10 MINUTES   **MAKES:** 4 SERVINGS

2   large sweet potatoes, peeled and sliced into ½-inch-thick rounds

¼   cup no-pulp orange juice

¼   cup chicken broth, store-bought or homemade (page 17)

Salt

5   cloves garlic, peeled

1   jalapeño, chopped

2   tablespoons olive oil

2   tablespoons ground cumin

1   teaspoon dried thyme

3   pounds bone-in, skinless chicken thighs

1   mango, peeled and cubed

1   avocado, peeled and cubed

1   tablespoon lime juice

1 In Instant Pot®, layer sweet potatoes. In bowl, mix together orange juice, chicken broth, and ¼ teaspoon salt; pour over potatoes. In processor, blend garlic, jalapeño, olive oil, cumin, and thyme into smooth paste.

2 Sprinkle chicken thighs with ¼ teaspoon salt. Arrange over sweet potatoes; spread with garlic mixture. Cover and set release valve to the venting position. Select Slow Cook and cook on high for 4 hours or low for 8 hours.

3 About 5 minutes before serving, in bowl, toss mango, avocado, lime juice, and pinch of salt. Serve chicken with sweet potatoes topped with salsa.

EACH SERVING: ABOUT 595 CALORIES, 44G PROTEIN, 53G CARBOHYDRATE, 24G TOTAL FAT (4G SATURATED), 10G FIBER, 625MG SODIUM.

TIP

Serve with a side of black beans and rice.

PRESSURE COOKER
Quicker Coq au Vin Blanc

Make this classic French recipe, with the same delicious flavor, in record time.

ACTIVE TIME: 10 MINUTES   **TOTAL TIME:** 35 MINUTES   **MAKES:** 4 SERVINGS

4   ounces pancetta, chopped

2   teaspoons olive oil

3   pounds assorted chicken pieces

½   teaspoon dried thyme

Salt

Freshly ground black pepper

1   medium leek, thinly sliced and well rinsed

1½   cups dry white wine

1   pound golden potatoes, cut into 1-inch chunks

12   ounces cremini mushrooms, quartered

Chopped fresh parsley, for garnish

1 In Instant Pot® using sauté function, cook pancetta in oil, uncovered, for 5 to 7 minutes, or until fat has rendered. Transfer pancetta to plate.

2 Meanwhile, pat chicken dry with paper towels; season all over with thyme and ½ teaspoon each salt and pepper.

3 In batches, add chicken, skin side down, to pot; cook 6 minutes or until browned on two sides, turning once halfway through. Transfer chicken to large plate.

4 To pot, add leek and ¼ teaspoon salt; cook 3 minutes, stirring. Add wine. Hit cancel, reselect sauté function, and adjust heat to More; heat to boiling. Hit cancel again, then reselect sauté function (this returns heat to Normal); simmer 5 minutes. Hit cancel to turn off sauté function.

5 Add potatoes, mushrooms, and chicken to pot. Cover and lock lid. Select Manual/Pressure Cook and cook at high pressure for 8 minutes. Once cooking is complete, release pressure by using a quick release.

6 Serve chicken and vegetables with some cooking liquid. Garnish with parsley.

EACH SERVING: ABOUT 725 CALORIES, 52G PROTEIN, 29G CARBOHYDRATE, 43G TOTAL FAT (13G SATURATED), 2G FIBER, 785MG SODIUM.

TIP

Here are a few Test Kitchen tricks to get that perfectly golden skin: Pat the skin very dry, and make sure the oil is hot but not smoking. Keep a little space between chicken parts when searing so you won't overcrowd the pan. You might have to do it in a couple of batches.

SLOW COOKER
Chicken with Walnut-Herb Sauce

Prepare this chicken over the weekend for use in meals throughout the week.

ACTIVE TIME: 40 MINUTES   **TOTAL TIME:** 4 HOURS, 40 MINUTES   **MAKES:** 6 SERVINGS

1   medium onion, cut into ½-inch slices

2   tablespoons olive oil

1   tablespoon ground coriander

¼   teaspoon ground cinnamon

Freshly ground black pepper

1   whole chicken (about 4 pounds)

Salt

⅔   cup walnuts, toasted

½   cup packed fresh mint leaves, plus more for garnish

¼   cup packed fresh basil leaves

1   tablespoon lemon juice

6   flatbreads, toasted

CABBAGE-KOHLRABI SLAW

4   cups thinly sliced red cabbage

2   small kohlrabi bulbs (see Tip), peeled and cut into matchsticks

1   seedless (English) cucumber, center removed, cut into matchsticks

½   cup packed fresh parsley

2   green onions, thinly sliced

¼   cup lemon juice

⅓   teaspoon salt

1 Arrange onion slices in single layer on bottom of Instant Pot®. In small bowl, combine oil, coriander, cinnamon, and ½ teaspoon black pepper; rub all over and inside chicken. With butcher's twine, tie drumsticks together. Sprinkle all over with ¾ teaspoon salt.

2 Place chicken on onion in pot. Cover and set release valve to the venting position. Select Slow Cook and cook on high for 4 hours.

3 While chicken is cooking, make Cabbage-Kohlrabi Slaw: Toss together red cabbage, kohlrabi (or jicama), cucumber, parsley, green onions, lemon juice, and salt.

4 Transfer chicken to cutting board. In blender, puree 1 cup liquid from pot with onion, walnuts, mint, basil, lemon juice, and ¼ teaspoon salt until smooth. Serve chicken with herb sauce, flatbreads, and Cabbage-Kohlrabi Slaw.

EACH SERVING: ABOUT 785 CALORIES, 45G PROTEIN, 54G CARBOHYDRATE, 44G FAT (11G SATURATED), 7G FIBER, 1,005MG SODIUM.

TIP

If you cannot find kohlrabi at your local supermarket, use 1 large jicama bulb instead.

Tangy BBQ Chicken

If you prefer a thicker sauce, boil it in a saucepan
to get the consistency you like.

ACTIVE TIME: 15 MINUTES   **TOTAL TIME:** 4 HOURS, 15 MINUTES   **MAKES:** 4 SERVINGS

1	cup ketchup
2	tablespoons spicy brown mustard
2	tablespoons balsamic vinegar
2	teaspoons Worcestershire sauce
1	clove garlic
1/4	teaspoons smoked paprika

Ground black pepper

4	bone-in chicken-breast halves, skin removed
4	chicken drumsticks, skin removed

Salt

Prepared coleslaw, for serving

1 Spray Instant Pot® bowl with nonstick cooking spray.

2 In medium bowl, with wire whisk, stir together ketchup, mustard, vinegar, Worcestershire sauce, garlic, smoked paprika, and $\frac{1}{8}$ teaspoon black pepper; transfer half of sauce to Instant Pot®.

3 Sprinkle chicken with $\frac{1}{2}$ teaspoon salt and $\frac{1}{4}$ teaspoon pepper; add to pot. Spoon remaining sauce over and around chicken to coat. Cover and set release valve to the venting position. Select Slow Cook and cook on high for 4 hours, or until chicken is no longer pink.

4 Transfer chicken to serving platter. Whisk cooking liquid until well mixed; drizzle over chicken. Serve chicken with coleslaw and any remaining sauce.

EACH SERVING: ABOUT 320 CALORIES, 44G PROTEIN, 18G CARBOHYDRATE, 7G TOTAL FAT (2G SATURATED), 0G FIBER, 1,275MG SODIUM.

Taco-Night Carnitas
(page 111)

5 Beef, Lamb & Pork

Both pressure cooking and slow cooking tenderize beef, pork, and lamb until they fall apart, therefore, this appliance is the answer to delicious meals in record time. Korean-spiced beef top round in Spicy Sesame Rice Bowls can be served in 35 minutes. Weeknight Tuscan Ragu will be on the table in a little over an hour. If you have more time, combine the ingredients for Pot Roast with Red Wine Sauce or Chipotle Pork and let the flavors develop over low heat for slow-cooked perfection. And if you need a meal to impress, Apricot-Braised Lamb Shanks will do just that. Either way, these recipes are delicious dinnertime solutions.

Weeknight Tuscan Ragu

Serve an Italian-style Sunday supper any day of the week with speed and ease using the pressure-cooker program on your Instant Pot®.

ACTIVE TIME: 15 MINUTES   **TOTAL TIME:** 1 HOUR, 10 MINUTES   **MAKES:** 8 SERVINGS

8   ounces sweet Italian sausage, casings removed

2   teaspoons olive oil

2½ pounds boneless pork shoulder, trimmed of excess fat and cut into 1-inch chunks

¾   teaspoon salt

½   teaspoon ground black pepper

2   medium carrots, finely chopped

1   medium onion, finely chopped

3   cloves garlic, chopped

1   cup dry red wine

1   can (28 ounces) crushed tomatoes

½   cup whole milk

3   bay leaves

½   cup packed fresh basil leaves, torn

1   pound pappardelle pasta, cooked according to package directions

Freshly grated Parmesan cheese, for serving

1 In Instant Pot® using sauté function, cook sausage in oil, uncovered, for 5 minutes, or until fat has rendered, breaking up meat as it cooks. With slotted spoon, transfer to large bowl.

2 Season pork all over with ½ teaspoon salt and pepper. In batches, add pork to pot; cook 4 minutes, or until browned on two sides, turning once halfway through. Transfer pork to bowl with sausage. To pot, add carrots, onion, and garlic; cook 8 minutes, stirring often. Add wine; cook 3 minutes. Hit cancel to turn off sauté function.

3 Return meat to pot and add tomatoes, milk, bay leaves, and remaining ¼ teaspoon salt. Cover and lock lid. Select Manual/Pressure Cook and cook at high pressure for 20 minutes. Once cooking is complete, release pressure by using natural release function.

4 Discard bay leaves and stir in basil. Toss with cooked pasta. Serve garnished with Parmesan.

EACH SERVING: ABOUT 550 CALORIES, 37G PROTEIN, 54G CARBOHYDRATE, 10G FAT (6G SATURATED), 5G FIBER, 500MG SODIUM.

Pot Roast with Red Wine Sauce

Classic French ingredients such as thyme, pearl onions, and red wine season this easy meal.

....

ACTIVE TIME: 25 MINUTES   **TOTAL TIME:** 2 HOURS, 30 MINUTES   **MAKES:** 8 SERVINGS

....

1   boneless beef chuck roast (3 to 3½ pounds)

Salt

Freshly ground black pepper

1   tablespoon vegetable oil

1   stalk celery, chopped

¾   cup dry red wine

1   can (14½ ounces) diced tomatoes

4   cloves garlic, smashed with side of chef's knife

½   teaspoon dried thyme

1   bay leaf

1   pound carrots, peeled and cut into 2-inch chunks

1   package (1 pound) frozen pearl onions

1   tablespoon cornstarch dissolved in 2 tablespoons water

1 Pat beef dry with paper towels; season on all sides with ¼ teaspoon each salt and pepper. In Instant Pot® select sauté function and adjust heat to More. Cook beef in oil for 6 minutes, until browned, turning once. Set on plate. Add celery and wine; cook 2 minutes. Stir in tomatoes, garlic, thyme, and bay leaf. Hit cancel to turn off sauté function.

2 Place beef on top and press into sauce. Cover and lock lid. Select Manual/Pressure Cook and cook at high pressure for 1 hour 15 minutes. Once cooking is complete, release pressure by using natural release function. Transfer beef to cutting board. Discard bay leaf.

3 Skim off any excess fat from surface. Choose sauté function and adjust heat to More. Cook 18 minutes, or until reduced by about half (2½ cups). Hit cancel to turn off sauté function.

4 Add carrots and onions. Cover and lock lid. Select Manual/Pressure Cook and cook at high pressure for 4 minutes. Once cooking is complete, release pressure by using a quick release. Using sauté function, keep at a simmer. Gradually stir in cornstarch mixture and cook 1 minute. Season with salt and pepper to taste.

5 Slice meat across the grain and serve with vegetables and sauce.

....

EACH SERVING: ABOUT 525 CALORIES, 45G PROTEIN, 15G CARBOHYDRATE, 30G TOTAL FAT (11G SATURATED), 3G FIBER, 318MG SODIUM.

SLOW COOKER
Ginger & Soy Short Ribs

Hours of cooking melts the fat off this cut of beef, creating a flavorful meatiness that holds its own against Asian spices.

ACTIVE TIME: 20 MINUTES **TOTAL TIME:** 10 HOURS, 20 MINUTES **MAKES:** 8 SERVINGS

4   pounds bone-in beef short ribs

Salt

Freshly ground black pepper

2   teaspoons vegetable oil

1   cup beef broth, store-bought or homemade (page 19)

2   tablespoons lower-sodium soy sauce

2   tablespoons balsamic vinegar

5   slices fresh ginger

3   tablespoons brown sugar

2   cloves garlic

3   star anise pods

Cooked brown rice, for serving

Steamed broccoli, for serving

Sesame seeds, for garnish

Green onions, chopped, for garnish

1 Sprinkle short ribs with ½ teaspoon each salt and pepper. In Instant Pot®, select sauté function and adjust heat to More. Add oil and when very hot, brown short ribs in batches, just on meaty sides.

2 Meanwhile, in bowl, whisk together beef broth, soy sauce, balsamic vinegar, ginger, brown sugar, garlic, and star anise.

3 Return all meat to Instant Pot® and add broth mixture. Cover and set release valve to the venting position. Select Slow Cook and cook on high for 5 hours or low for 10 hours, or until very tender. Transfer meat to cutting board.

4 Skim and discard fat from cooking liquid. Choose sauté function and adjust heat to More. Heat to boiling and cook 5 to 10 minutes, or until reduced by about half.

5 Discard ginger, garlic cloves, and star anise. Serve meat with brown rice and broccoli. Drizzle meat with reduced sauce; garnish with sesame seeds and green onion slices.

EACH SERVING (SHORT RIBS ONLY): ABOUT 560 CALORIES, 25G PROTEIN, 6G CARBOHYDRATE, 48G TOTAL FAT (20G SATURATED), 0G FIBER, 485MG SODIUM.

SLOW COOKER
Pulled BBQ Beef

Kick up midweek dinners with this intense smoky-sweet barbecue sauce. A quick sear on the short ribs before slow cooking adds more prep and develops richer flavor.

ACTIVE TIME: 20 MINUTES **TOTAL TIME:** 10 HOURS, 20 MINUTES **MAKES:** 6 SERVINGS

4   pounds bone-in beef short ribs

Salt

Freshly ground black pepper

2   teaspoons vegetable oil

1   cup ketchup

2   tablespoons spicy brown mustard

1   tablespoon Worcestershire sauce

3   tablespoons red wine vinegar

1   teaspoon smoked paprika

¾   teaspoon crushed red pepper flakes

¼   teaspoon onion powder

3   cups slaw mix

6 hamburger buns, for serving

1 Sprinkle short ribs with ½ teaspoon each salt and pepper. In Instant Pot®, select sauté function and adjust heat to More. Add oil and when very hot, brown short ribs in batches, just on meaty sides.

2 Meanwhile, in bowl, whisk together ketchup, mustard, Worcestershire sauce, 1 tablespoon vinegar, smoked paprika, ¼ teaspoon pepper flakes, and onion powder.

3 Return all meat to Instant Pot® and add ketchup mixture. Cover and set release valve to the venting position. Select Slow Cook and cook on high for 5 hours or low for 10 hours, or until very tender. Transfer meat to cutting board.

4 Skim and discard fat from cooking liquid. Choose sauté function and adjust heat to More. Heat to boiling and cook 5 to 10 minutes, or until reduced by about half.

5 With hands, shred meat, discarding fat, bones, and gristle. Return meat to pot with reduced sauce; toss until well coated.

6 In large bowl, toss slaw mix with remaining 2 tablespoons vinegar, ½ teaspoon pepper flakes, and 1/8 teaspoon salt.

7 Serve meat on buns with slaw.

EACH SERVING (WITHOUT BUN): ABOUT 400 CALORIES, 29G PROTEIN, 31G CARBOHYDRATE, 16G TOTAL FAT (7G SATURATED), 2G FIBER, 835MG SODIUM.

Tex-Mex Beef Sammies

This super-easy, tender beef will be the fan favorite at your next party.
Pile it high on a baguette and serve them up!

ACTIVE TIME: 10 MINUTES   **TOTAL TIME:** 1 HOUR, 25 MINUTES   **MAKES:** 12 SERVINGS

3   pounds boneless beef chuck roast, trimmed

2   tablespoons chili powder

1   can (10 ounces) diced tomatoes with green chiles

1   can (4 ounces) chopped green chiles

½   cup light mayonnaise

3   green onions, finely chopped

2   tablespoons lime juice

Sandwich rolls, for serving

Lettuce, for serving

1   Rub beef with chili powder. Pour diced tomatoes into Instant Pot®. Add beef and top with green chiles. Cover and lock lid. Select Manual/Pressure Cook and cook at high pressure for 1 hour 15 minutes. Once cooking is complete, release pressure by using a quick release.

2   In small bowl, combine mayonnaise, green onions, and lime juice. Slice or shred beef, discarding any fat. Serve on sandwich rolls with lettuce and lime mayonnaise.

EACH SERVING: ABOUT 420 CALORIES, 22G PROTEIN, 30G CARBOHYDRATE, 21G TOTAL FAT (8G SATURATED), 2G FIBER, 527MG SODIUM.

French Dip Brisket Reuben Sandwiches

Sauerkraut, a fermented cabbage condiment,
is a good source of probiotics for a healthy gut.

ACTIVE TIME: 10 MINUTES TOTAL TIME: 8 HOURS, 10 MINUTES MAKES: 6 SERVINGS

1 small beef brisket (about 2½ pounds), trimmed and cut into 3 pieces

2 medium onions, sliced

4 cloves garlic, crushed with garlic press

1 can (14 ounces) beef broth or 1¾ cups homemade (page 19)

3 tablespoons soy sauce

6 rolls, split

¾ cup sauerkraut, drained

6 slices Swiss cheese

1 Place beef brisket, onions, garlic, beef broth, and soy sauce in Instant Pot®. Cover and set release valve to the venting position. Select Slow Cook and cook on low for 7 to 8 hours, or until very tender.

2 Pull meat apart with fork; place on rolls and top each with 2 tablespoons sauerkraut and 1 slice cheese. Broil just until melted. Replace tops of rolls. Serve with cooking liquid for dipping, if desired.

EACH SERVING: ABOUT 450 CALORIES, 47G PROTEIN, 27G CARBOHYDRATE, 17G TOTAL FAT (7G SATURATED), 2G FIBER, 600MG SODIUM.

SLOW COOKER
Brisket with Roasted Red Onions

This tender family favorite, roasted to garlicky perfection with tomatoes and onions, requires only a handful of pantry staples.

ACTIVE TIME: 10 MINUTES **TOTAL TIME:** 10 HOURS, 10 MINUTES **MAKES:** 6 SERVINGS

4   pounds beef brisket, trimmed

Salt

Freshly ground black pepper

1   can (14 ounces) crushed tomatoes

3   cloves garlic, crushed with garlic press

1   medium red onion, sliced

1   medium yellow onion, sliced

1   tablespoon olive oil

Finely chopped fresh parsley, for garnish

1 Season brisket with ¾ teaspoon each salt and pepper; add to Instant Pot® along with crushed tomatoes and garlic. Cover and set release valve to the venting position. Select Slow Cook and cook on low for 10 hours, or until very tender.

2 About 1 hour before meat is ready, preheat oven to 425°F. On large rimmed baking sheet, toss onions with olive oil and ¼ teaspoon salt. Roast 20 minutes, or until browned.

3 Serve brisket topped with roasted onions and chopped parsley.

EACH SERVING: ABOUT 300 CALORIES, 35G PROTEIN, 9G CARBOHYDRATE, 14G TOTAL FAT (4G SATURATED), 2G FIBER, 590MG SODIUM.

SLOW COOKER
Cuban-Style Beef

This heart-healthy and low-calorie Latin-inspired recipe
will awaken your taste buds.

ACTIVE TIME: 30 MINUTES **TOTAL TIME:** 10 HOURS, 30 MINUTES **MAKES:** 12 SERVINGS

1   boneless beef chuck roast (about 4 pounds)

1   teaspoon dried oregano

1   teaspoon ground cumin

Salt

Freshly ground black pepper

2   teaspoons vegetable oil

1   large onion

1   large green bell pepper

1   large red bell pepper

2   cloves garlic

1   can (28 ounces) crushed tomatoes

½   cup pimiento-stuffed green olives, sliced

Chopped fresh parsley, for garnish (optional)

1 Rub roast with oregano, cumin, and
½ teaspoon each salt and pepper. In Instant
Pot®, select sauté function and adjust heat to
More. Add oil and when very hot add roast
and brown on all sides. Transfer to plate.

2 To pot, add onion, bell peppers, garlic,
2 tablespoons water, and ¼ teaspoon salt; cook,
uncovered, for 2 to 4 minutes, or until slightly
softened, stirring. Add crushed tomatoes.
Simmer 4 minutes, stirring. Hit cancel to turn
off sauté function.

3 Nestle roast into sauce and spoon sauce over
meat. Cover and set release valve to the venting
position. Select Slow Cook and cook on low for
10 hours, or until tender.

4 Shred meat (discard fat and gristle). With
slotted spoon, transfer vegetables to large serving
bowl. Stir in meat, pimiento-stuffed green olives,
and ¼ teaspoon salt. Garnish with parsley, if
desired.

EACH SERVING: ABOUT 245 CALORIES, 33G PROTEIN,
9G CARBOHYDRATE, 8G TOTAL FAT (3G SATURATED),
2G FIBER, 435MG SODIUM.

TIP

This delicious beef dish can be served with
saffron-spiked yellow rice or Coconut Rice
(page 39).

SLOW COOKER
Cajun Beef & Grits

This comfort food dish, straight out of N'awlins, has true grit—literally.

ACTIVE TIME: 30 MINUTES   **TOTAL TIME:** 7 HOURS, 40 MINUTES   **MAKES:** 8 SERVINGS

2   teaspoons canola oil

3½ pounds boneless beef chuck, trimmed and cut into 1-inch chunks

Salt

3   medium bell peppers, chopped

1   large onion, chopped

3   stalks celery, chopped

3   cloves garlic, chopped

1   can (14 ounces) diced tomatoes, drained

¼   cup tomato paste

2   teaspoons Cajun or Creole seasoning

2   cups grits (see Tip)

2   cups shredded sharp Cheddar cheese

Freshly ground black pepper

Finely chopped fresh parsley, for garnish

1 In Instant Pot®, select sauté function, adjust heat to More, and heat oil. Pat beef dry with paper towels; season all over with ½ teaspoon salt. In batches, cook beef 5 minutes, or until browned on two sides. Transfer to a plate.

2 Hit cancel, then reselect sauté function (this returns heat to Normal). Add bell peppers, onion, celery, and garlic. Cook, uncovered, for 3 minutes, stirring. Add diced tomatoes and tomato paste; cook 2 minutes, stirring. Stir in Cajun seasoning. Return beef to pot; stir to combine. Cover and set release valve to the venting position. Select Slow Cook and cook on low for 7 hours, or until beef is very tender.

3 About 1 hour before ready to serve, in covered 5- to 6-quart saucepot, heat 10 cups of water and ¾ teaspoon salt to boiling on high. Slowly whisk in grits. Reduce heat to maintain simmer. Cook 30 to 40 minutes, or until grits are tender, whisking often. Remove from heat. Stir in Cheddar and ¾ teaspoon black pepper.

4 Serve beef and vegetables over grits. Garnish with parsley.

EACH SERVING: ABOUT 555 CALORIES, 45G PROTEIN, 45G CARBOHYDRATE, 23G FAT (10G SATURATED), 4G FIBER, 750MG SODIUM.

TIP

No grits on-hand? Try polenta but be sure to adjust the amount of water (check the label). It cooks up a little differently.

Spicy Sesame Rice Bowls

Gochujang (Korean red pepper paste) gives this healthy recipe tons of flavor—pressure cooking just makes it easy.

ACTIVE TIME: 25 MINUTES **TOTAL TIME:** 35 MINUTES **MAKES:** 6 SERVINGS

⅓ cup gochujang (Korean red pepper paste)

2 tablespoons toasted sesame oil

1 tablespoon soy sauce

1 tablespoon sugar

3 cloves garlic, crushed with garlic press

1 pound beef top round, cut across grain into very thin 2-inch-long slices

Salt

12 ounces shiitake mushrooms, stemmed

1 seedless (English) cucumber, thinly sliced

¼ cup rice vinegar

5 ounces baby spinach

6 cups freshly cooked white rice

Thinly sliced green onions, shredded carrots, kimchi, and sesame seeds, for serving

1 In large bowl, whisk together gochujang, sesame oil, soy sauce, sugar, garlic, and ¼ cup water until smooth; set aside ½ cup sauce. To bowl with remaining sauce, add beef and a pinch salt, tossing to coat. Let stand at least 10 minutes or refrigerate, covered, up to overnight.

2 Add beef to Instant Pot® along with mushrooms. Cover and lock lid. Select Manual/Pressure Cook and cook at high pressure for 10 minutes. Once cooking is complete, release pressure by using a quick release.

3 While beef cooks, toss cucumber with vinegar and ¼ teaspoon salt; set aside.

4 Divide spinach among 6 serving bowls; top each with 1 cup rice. Drain cucumbers. Top rice with beef, mushrooms, cucumbers, green onions, carrots, kimchi, and sesame seeds; drizzle with sauce in pot.

EACH SERVING: ABOUT 450 CALORIES, 26G PROTEIN, 65G CARBOHYDRATE, 10G FAT (2G SATURATED), 5G FIBER, 710MG SODIUM.

TIP

Kimchi is a Korean spicy pickled cabbage. Look for it in the refrigerated section of your grocery store, near the tofu. If you can't find it, you might need to check a specialty food store.

SLOW COOKER
Sweet & Tangy Braised Roast

Gingersnap crumbs and raisins give this classic roast a sweet treatment.

ACTIVE TIME: 10 MINUTES   **TOTAL TIME:** 10 HOURS, 10 MINUTES   **MAKES:** 6 SERVINGS

6 gingersnap cookies, finely crushed into crumbs

2 cups peeled baby carrots

2 large stalks celery, cut crosswise into 2-inch pieces

1 medium onion, cut into 1-inch pieces

1 cup dry red wine

2 tablespoons red wine vinegar

¼ cup raisins

1 teaspoon salt

½ teaspoon ground black pepper

1 boneless beef chuck roast (about 2 pounds)

1 In Instant Pot®, combine gingersnap crumbs, carrots, celery, onion, wine, vinegar, raisins, salt, and pepper.

2 Place roast on top of vegetables. Cover and set release valve to the venting position. Select Slow Cook and cook on high for 6 to 6½ hours or low for 8 to 10 hours, or until roast is very tender.

3 Place roast on warm platter. Skim and discard fat from cooking liquid. Serve roast with vegetables and sauce.

EACH SERVING: ABOUT 360 CALORIES, 25G PROTEIN, 27G CARBOHYDRATE, 21G TOTAL FAT (8G SATURATED), 2G FIBER, 540MG SODIUM.

TIP

Less tender cuts of meat like chuck roast aren't just lower in cost, they are especially well suited for slow cooking or pressure cooking.

SLOW COOKER
Taco-Night Carnitas

Serve this meal family-style and let dinner guests assemble their own tacos. For photo, see page 90.

ACTIVE TIME: 20 MINUTES   **TOTAL TIME:** 7 HOURS, 20 MINUTES   **MAKES:** 8 SERVINGS

1   tablespoon canola oil

4   pounds boneless pork shoulder, trimmed of excess fat and cut into 3 pieces

2   tablespoons ground cumin

Salt

1   large white onion, chopped

3   poblano chiles, seeded and chopped

2   serrano chiles, sliced

4   cloves garlic, crushed with garlic press

½   cup chicken broth (store-bought or homemade, page 17) or water

¼   cup lime juice

24   small tortillas, warmed (see Tip)

Cilantro, sliced green onions, sliced radishes, salsa, and lime wedges, for serving

1 In Instant Pot® select sauté function, adjust heat to More, and heat oil. Season pork all over with cumin and 1 teaspoon salt. Cook 5 minutes, or until browned on two sides, turning over once halfway through. Transfer pork to a plate.

2 To pot, add onion, chiles, and garlic; cook 2 minutes, stirring often. Hit cancel to turn off sauté function.

3 Add broth, lime juice, and pork to pot. Cover and set release valve to the venting position. Select Slow Cook and cook on low for 7 hours, or until very tender.

4 Transfer pork to cutting board; with two forks, pull into bite-size shreds, discarding any fat. Serve with tortillas and fixings.

EACH SERVING: ABOUT 430 CALORIES, 36G PROTEIN, 38G CARBOHYDRATE, 14G FAT (4G SATURATED), 7G FIBER, 430MG SODIUM.

TIP

Want to warm up your tortillas? Use a dry nonstick skillet over medium heat to toast each tortilla on both sides until it's browned in spots. Wrap first in a damp paper towel, then in foil to keep soft and warm.

New Mexican Green Chile Pork

Tomatillos, used to make this green chile pork, grow inside a papery husk. They are available from May through November.

ACTIVE TIME: 25 MINUTES   **TOTAL TIME:** 8 HOURS, 25 MINUTES   **MAKES:** 6 SERVINGS

1   bone-in pork shoulder roast (about 4 pounds)

1   tablespoon chipotle chile powder

1   tablespoon brown sugar

Salt

Freshly ground black pepper

2   pounds fresh tomatillos

1   jumbo white onion

4   cloves garlic

3   jalapeños

½   cup packed fresh cilantro with stems

⅓   cup lower-sodium chicken broth, store-bought or homemade (page 17)

3   cups cooked brown rice

Lime wedges

1   Preheat broiler with oven rack 6 inches from heat source. Line an 18 x 12-inch rimmed baking sheet with foil.

2   Place pork in Instant Pot®. In small bowl, combine chipotle powder, brown sugar, 1 teaspoon salt, and ½ teaspoon black pepper. Rub all over pork in pot.

3   On prepared baking sheet, spread tomatillos, onion, garlic, and jalapeños in a single layer. Broil 7 minutes, or until blackened and blistered in spots, stirring twice. Immediately add to pot along with cilantro and broth. Cover and set release valve to the venting position. Select Slow Cook and cook on low for 8 hours.

4   With tongs and large serving spoon, transfer pork to cutting board. Remove and discard bone and excess fat. Cut off one-third of meat; transfer to container and refrigerate up to 3 days (see Tip). With large serving spoon, transfer all vegetables to blender. Puree until smooth. Thin with additional cooking liquid if desired. Transfer half of sauce to container (refrigerate up to 3 days). Discard remaining liquid in Instant Pot®.

5   Cut remaining pork in slices across grain. Serve with rice and lime wedges. Spoon remaining sauce over pork and garnish with cilantro.

EACH SERVING: ABOUT 440 CALORIES, 29G PROTEIN, 34G CARBOHYDRATE, 21G TOTAL FAT (7G SATURATED), 5G FIBER, 350MG SODIUM.

TIP

Use the reserved items (⅓ of the meat and ¼ of the sauce) to make tacos for an easy weekday meal.

SLOW COOKER
Chipotle Pork

As easy as set it and forget it, this super-flavorful pork recipe can be ready when you walk in the door.

ACTIVE TIME: 15 MINUTES TOTAL TIME: 9 HOURS, 15 MINUTES MAKES: 8 SERVINGS

1   medium onion, peeled and cut into chunks

½   cup chicken broth, store-bought or homemade (page 17)

½   cup ketchup

¼   cup chipotles in adobo sauce

¼   cup creamy peanut butter

5   cloves garlic, peeled

2   tablespoons unsweetened cocoa

1   teaspoon salt

1   boneless pork shoulder (about 3 to 4 pounds), trimmed of excess fat

Cooked curly egg noodles, for serving

Orange wedges

Green onions, thinly sliced

1 In food processor, puree onion, broth, ketchup, chipotles, peanut butter, garlic, and cocoa until smooth. Sprinkle salt all over pork shoulder; place in Instant Pot®. Pour onion mixture over pork. Cover and set release valve to the venting position. Select Slow Cook and cook on high for 5 to 6 hours or low for 8 to 9 hours, until pork is tender but not falling apart.

2 Transfer pork to cutting board. Pour sauce into fat separator. When pork is cool enough to handle, remove and discard fat. Pull pork into bite-size chunks. Serve over curly egg noodles along with sauce. Garnish with orange wedges and green onions.

EACH SERVING: ABOUT 300 CALORIES, 26G PROTEIN, 14G CARBOHYDRATE, 16G TOTAL FAT (5G SATURATED), 3G FIBER, 655MG SODIUM.

PRESSURE COOKER
Apricot-Braised Lamb Shanks

Lamb shanks braised with orange juice, tomatoes, honey, and raisins emerge from the pressure cooker falling-off-the-bone tender.

ACTIVE TIME: 15 MINUTES   **TOTAL TIME:** 1 HOUR   **MAKES:** 4 SERVINGS

4	lamb shanks (about 4 pounds total)
1	teaspoon salt
1/4	teaspoon ground black pepper
2	tablespoons all-purpose flour
2	tablespoons olive oil
1	medium onion, chopped
1	tablespoon grated peeled fresh ginger
2	cloves garlic, crushed with garlic press
1	can (14½ ounces) diced tomatoes
3	carrots, cut into 1½-inch chunks
1/2	cup dried apricots
1/2	cup raisins
1/2	cup fresh orange juice
1/4	cup honey

1 Season lamb shanks with ½ teaspoon salt and ⅛ teaspoon pepper and dredge in flour.

2 In Instant Pot® using sauté function, heat oil. Add shanks, two at a time, and cook 5 minutes per side, or until browned. Transfer to plate. Add onion to pot and cook 3 minutes, or until softened, stirring occasionally. Stir in ginger and garlic and cook 1 minute. Hit cancel to turn off sauté function.

3 Return shanks to pot and add tomatoes, carrots, apricots, and raisins. In cup, stir together orange juice, honey, and remaining ½ teaspoon salt and ⅛ teaspoon pepper. Pour over shanks. Cover and lock lid. Select Manual/Pressure Cook and cook at high pressure for 35 minutes. Once cooking is complete, release pressure by using natural release function.

4 Serve shanks with pan sauce.

EACH SERVING: ABOUT 755 CALORIES, 45G PROTEIN, 63G CARBOHYDRATE, 36G TOTAL FAT (14G SATURATED), 5G FIBER, 1,008MG SODIUM.

TIP

The lamb shanks pair nicely with our Parsley & Lemon Chickpeas (page 32).

Korean Pork Lettuce Wraps

Radishes and cucumbers are used as garnishes and
add coolness to the spicy meal made with gochujang.

ACTIVE TIME: 10 MINUTES   **TOTAL TIME:** 1 HOUR, 10 MINUTES   **MAKES:** 8 SERVINGS

¼   cup miso

¼   cup lower-sodium soy sauce

3   tablespoons gochujang (Korean red pepper paste) or Sriracha sauce, plus more for serving

1   tablespoon toasted sesame oil

1   teaspoon ground black pepper

1   boneless pork shoulder (about 4 pounds), trimmed of excess fat and quartered

Lettuce leaves, for serving

Thinly sliced radishes, cucumber, and green onions, for serving

1 In small bowl, whisk together miso, soy sauce, ¼ cup water, gochujang, sesame oil, and black pepper until smooth.

2 Pour half of sauce into Instant Pot®. Add pork and pour remaining sauce over top. Cover and lock lid. Select Manual/Pressure Cook and cook at high pressure for 1 hour. Once cooking is complete, release pressure by using a quick release.

3 Shred pork and serve in lettuce leaves with radishes, cucumbers, green onions, and additional gochujang or Sriracha.

EACH SERVING (PORK ONLY): ABOUT 450 CALORIES, 53G PROTEIN, 6G CARBOHYDRATE, 21G FAT (7G SATURATED), 1G FIBER, 784MG SODIUM.

Tuscan Pork with Fennel

Fennel is an aromatic vegetable used in Mediterranean cooking and tastes similar to anise or licorice. This recipe utilizes the seeds in a rub and braises the vegetable as a side.

ACTIVE TIME: 25 MINUTES   **TOTAL TIME:** 10 HOURS, 25 MINUTES   **MAKES:** 12 SERVINGS

2   teaspoons fennel seeds

1   teaspoon dried rosemary

Salt

Freshly ground black pepper

1   boneless pork shoulder (about 4 to 5 pounds), trimmed of excess fat and cut into quarters

¾   cup chicken broth, store-bought or homemade (page 17)

2   teaspoons chicken broth base or demi-glace

2   pounds red potatoes

2   medium fennel bulbs (fronds reserved for garnish)

3   cloves garlic

1 In small bowl, combine fennel seeds, rosemary, and ½ teaspoon each salt and pepper. Season pork shoulder with rub mixture.

2 In Instant Pot®, whisk together chicken broth, base or demi-glace, and ¼ teaspoon each salt and pepper; add potatoes, fennel, and garlic. Place pork on top of vegetables. Cover and set release valve to the venting position. Select Slow Cook and cook on high for 7 hours or low for 10 hours, or until very tender.

3 Transfer meat to cutting board. Skim and discard fat from cooking liquid.

4 Slice pork and serve with vegetables. Drizzle with cooking liquid. Garnish with chopped fennel fronds, if desired.

EACH SERVING: ABOUT 355 CALORIES, 29G PROTEIN, 104G CARBOHYDRATE, 19G FAT (7G SATURATED), 3G FIBER, 350MG SODIUM.

SLOW COOKER
Teriyaki Ribs

For a quick DIY teriyaki, simmer together ½ cup lower-sodium soy sauce, 2 tablespoons rice vinegar, and ¼ cup brown sugar.

ACTIVE TIME: 15 MINUTES   **TOTAL TIME:** 7 HOURS, 15 MINUTES   **MAKES:** 4 SERVINGS

1   large rack baby back ribs (2½ pounds), cut into pairs

½   teaspoon ground black pepper

2/3   cup teriyaki sauce

1   tablespoon balsamic vinegar

2   cloves garlic, crushed in garlic press

Slaw, for serving

Sesame seeds, for garnish (optional)

1 Sprinkle baby back ribs with pepper; place in Instant Pot® with ⅓ cup teriyaki sauce. Cover and set release valve to the venting position. Select Slow Cook and cook on high for 4 hours or low for 7 hours, or until tender.

2 Remove ribs from pot and cut ribs apart. In Instant Pot®, using sauté function simmer remaining ⅓ cup teriyaki sauce, balsamic vinegar, and garlic, uncovered, on medium-high 5 minutes. Brush glaze onto cooked ribs.

3 Serve with slaw. Garnish with sesame seeds, if desired.

EACH SERVING (WITH SLAW): ABOUT 495 CALORIES, 30G PROTEIN, 20G CARBOHYDRATE, 32G FAT (11G SATURATED), 1G FIBER, 1,100MG SODIUM.

Index

Note: Page references in *italics* indicate photographs.

Photography Credits

Metric Conversion Charts

The recipes that appear in this cookbook use the standard United States method for measuring liquid and dry or solid ingredients (teaspoons, tablespoons, and cups). The information on this chart is provided to help cooks outside the U.S. successfully use these recipes. All equivalents are approximate.

METRIC EQUIVALENTS FOR DIFFERENT TYPES OF INGREDIENTS

STANDARD CUP (e.g., flour)	FINE POWDER (e.g., rice)	GRAIN (e.g., sugar)	GRANULAR (e.g., butter)	LIQUID SOLIDS (e.g., milk)	LIQUID
¾	105 g	113 g	143 g	150 g	180 ml
⅔	93 g	100 g	125 g	133 g	160 ml
½	70 g	75 g	95 g	100 g	120 ml
⅓	47 g	50 g	63 g	67 g	80 ml
¼	35 g	38 g	48 g	50 g	60 ml
⅛	18 g	19 g	24 g	25 g	30 ml

USEFUL EQUIVALENTS FOR LIQUID INGREDIENTS BY VOLUME

¼ tsp	=						1 ml
½ tsp	=						2 ml
1 tsp	=						5 ml
3 tsp	=	1 tbsp	=		½ fl oz	=	15 ml
		2 tbsp	=	⅛ cup	=	1 fl oz	=	30 ml
		4 tbsp	=	¼ cup	=	2 fl oz	=	60 ml
		5⅓ tbsp	=	⅓ cup	=	3 fl oz	=	80 ml
		8 tbsp	=	½ cup	=	4 fl oz	=	120 ml
		10⅔ tbsp	=	⅔ cup	=	5 fl oz	=	160 ml
		12 tbsp	=	¾ cup	=	6 fl oz	=	180 ml
		16 tbsp	=	1 cup	=	8 fl oz	=	240 ml
		1 pt	=	2 cups	=	16 fl oz	=	480 ml
		1 qt	=	4 cups	=	32 fl oz	=	960 ml
					33 fl oz	=	1000 ml = 1 L

USEFUL EQUIVALENTS FOR DRY INGREDIENTS BY WEIGHT

(To convert ounces to grams, multiply the number of ounces by 30.)

1 oz	=	⅟₁₆ lb	=	30 g
2 oz	=	¼ lb	=	120 g
4 oz	=	½ lb	=	240 g
8 oz	=	¾ lb	=	360 g
16 oz	=	1 lb	=	480 g

USEFUL EQUIVALENTS FOR COOKING/OVEN TEMPERATURES

	Fahrenheit	Celsius	Gas Mark
Freeze Water	32°F	0°C	
Room Temperature	68°F	20°C	
Boil Water	212°F	100°C	
Bake	325°F	160°C	3
	350°F	180°C	4
	375°F	190°C	5
	400°F	200°C	6
	425°F	220°C	7
	450°F	230°C	8
Broil			Grill

USEFUL EQUIVALENTS LENGTH

(To convert inches to centimeters, multiply the number of inches by 2.5.)

1 in	=				2.5 cm	
6 in	=	½ ft	=		15 cm	
12 in	=	1 ft	=		30 cm	
36 in	=	3 ft	=	1 yd	=	90 cm
40 in	=				100 cm	= 1 m

THE GOOD HOUSEKEEPING
TRIPLE-TEST PROMISE

At *Good Housekeeping*, we want to make sure that every recipe we print works in any oven, with any brand of ingredient, no matter what. That's why, in our test kitchens at the **Good Housekeeping Research Institute**, we go all out: We test each recipe at least three times—and, often, several more times after that.

When a recipe is first developed, one member of our team prepares the dish, and we judge it on these criteria: It must be **delicious**, **family-friendly**, **healthy**, and **easy to make**.

1 The recipe is then tested several more times to fine-tune the flavor and ease of preparation, always by the same team member, using the same equipment.

2 Next, another team member follows the recipe as written, **varying the brands of ingredients** and **kinds of equipment**. Even the types of stoves we use are changed.

3 A third team member repeats the whole process **using yet another set of equipment** and **alternative ingredients**. By the time the recipes appear on these pages, they are guaranteed to work in any kitchen, including yours. **We promise**.